Drugs Make You Un-Smarter

By Savanna Peterson
and Jill Vanderwood
Cover Photo: JayLynn Photograpy
Illustrated by
Alex Sepulveda
Printed by Brighton's Mountain Books

Copyright 2011 Savanna J. Peterson and Jill A. Vanderwood
Printed by Brighton's Mountain Books
All rights reserved

No part of this publication may be reproduced, stored in a retrieval system, or transmitted in any form, or by any means, electronic, mechanical, photocopying, recording, or otherwise, without the written permission of the authors, except for brief passages embodied in critical articles and reviews.

This book is a work of nonfiction. All information submitted to or quoted by the authors is correct to the best of the author's knowledge. Some names and minor circumstances have been changed to protect the identity of those interviewed herein.

ISBN Number: 978-0615595412
Printed in the United States of America
Cover Format: Clark Stewart
Book Format: Why Wait Webs

The phrase "You don't know what you have till it's gone" has a lot of meaning to it. I didn't realize this until I lost someone very close to me on July 3rd, 2010, from a car crash. All my most joyful memories involve Tyler Blais, and it's very hard to accept the fact that I lost a friend and I can't ever have him back. Tyler lived his life drug-free and vegan. He had the most incredible hopes and desires. He made everyone around him feel welcomed and wanted. I still see visions in my head of Tyler sitting on a chair near the campfires we used to have on the weekends, singing his silly country songs and making everyone laugh. Tyler was always the entertainer and made the room light up when he walked in. His soul was pure and he was an angel. This was a huge loss. My friend, you are in God's arms now, looking down on us. I won't ever forget such an incredible kid. Tyler Jordan Blais, I dedicate this book to you, hon. SJP

Acknowledgements

We would like to thank Judi Shervell, Coordinator, Foundation for a Drug-Free World, for sending us information and writing a review. Tom Brennan of Tom Brennan Media, for putting us in contact with actor Jason London. Thank you, Sherriff Tom Allman from Face 2Face; Glen Purdie from Kiwanis, Judge Forrest W. Burt, Chrissy Kinch from Regan Communications for putting us in touch with Dr. Kishore; school counselor Jaye Gittleman and teachers Anela Deardon and Cassy Steinmiller for running class surveys; Dea Shandera Film, Media and Management Consultant, for putting us in touch with Author Kristen Moeller; Cyrus Webb for putting us in touch with actor/author Tray Cheney, Kae Tienstra, KT Public Relations & Literary Services for putting us in touch with author Jennifer Storm; and Ryan Foster from Sam's Club Pharmacy. Thank you Dominic Friesen Partner Bridge & Tunnel Communications for putting us in touch with Sherry Gaba LCSW, Life Coach and Psychotherapist; and Sherry Gaba for her willingness to be interviewed and referring us to Scott Gaba and Rebecca Kanefsky.

We also wish to thank our family for their help and participation, and all those who have willingly submitted their stories. We know this was often a tough and even soul-searching decision.

Drugs Make You Un-Smarter

Hello,

My name is Jill Ammon Vanderwood. I am an author and a grandmother. Last summer, I told two of my granddaughters I would help them write a book, thinking they would write a simple picture book with either illustrations or photos. A few days later, my fifteen-year-old granddaughter, Savanna, came to me and said, "I know what I want to write about. I want to write a book telling kids that even if someone in their family is doing drugs or drinking, they don't have to."

I was very surprised, but I told her I would help her. I bought her a notebook so she could start writing her story. I also told her that even if I was in the middle of something, when she was ready to write this book, I would drop everything and help her.

This book begins with Savanna's story. We go into sections which tell about various drugs and alcohol. In each section, you will find stories of people who have experienced effects of the drug. In the rehab section, we have interviews with doctors and those who have detoxed in rehabs, such as Savanna's cousin, Dillon, who has been down the hard road of drugs, been locked up as well as spending six weeks at a wilderness program, having a no-contact order with his cousin, Savanna's brother—even at Christmas time, and finally having a no-contact order with his own girlfriend. We include stories about Dillon's father who died a drug-related death, and his mother, who was hooked on crystal meth.

Learn about kids who say no to drugs, and celebrities who are taking a stand against drugs.

The reader will hear Savanna's compelling voice throughout this book, warning and pleading for kids to stay off drugs, get an education, and make a good life for themselves. Dillon once asked, "What could Savanna have to say about drugs? She has never been on drugs."

My answer is, "What doesn't she have to say?" From the time she was five years old, Savanna has been exposed to drugs, such as heroin. She cried in her room when she smelled weed coming from the bathroom, and whenever her mom came home drunk.

Savanna is a strong voice for youth. She has taken a stand against drugs, and encourages kids everywhere to Say No to Drugs and Say Yes to Life!

Table of Contents:

The Purpose of this book	Jill Vanderwood	5
Introduction: Be Strong	Savanna Peterson	12

Section 1
Savanna's Story:

When I Came Into the World	Savanna Peterson with Jill Vanderwood	15
My Dad	Savanna with Grandma Peterson	18
My Mom	Savanna Peterson with Jill Vanderwood	20
My Brother	Savanna Peterson	22
Things That Have Disappeared From My House	Savanna Peterson	26
My Dad Taught Me How to Steal	Savanna Peterson	27
What I Believe: Being Straight Edge	Savanna Peterson	29
The Heroes in My Life	Savanna Peterson	34

Section 2
How Drugs Affect a Family

Cold Turkey	An Interview with Brandon	37
A Tragic Turn of Events	Elizabeth	39
I Just Want My Dad Back	Jessica	43
A Case of Mistaken Identity	An Interview with Actor Jason London	44
The Power of Forgiveness	Brooks Gibbs--Teen Motivational Speaker	48

Section 3
Alcohol

The Dangers of Alcohol Use in Adolescents		54
Common Myths		54
What Happens to Your Body?		54
Signs of Alcohol Poisoning	College Drinking website	55
About Drunk Driving	Judge Forrest W. Burt	55
It's Always Going to Haunt Me	Dez	56
The Other Side of Alcoholism	Jill Vanderwood	59

Signs of Alcoholism	Jill Vanderwood	64
What Should I Do If I've Been Drinking?	Jill Vanderwood	66

Section 4
Marijuana

Facts about Marijuana		68
Mentally Obsessed	Tina	69
Just Pot?	Ryan Frazier	72
When I Grow Up	Jennifer Parker	75

Section 5
Crack

What Are the Signs of Drug Addiction?	Brooks Gibbs - Teen Motivational Speaker	79
Facts about Crack Cocaine		80
I Was Addicted Before I Took My First Hit	Jennifer Storm	82
Disneyland	Rebecca Kanefsky	84
Everything to Lose	Britney Campbell	88

Section 6
Cocaine

Facts about Cocaine		92
The Coke Man	Rebecca Kanefsky	93
I Overdosed Twice	Erica Catton	97
Losing Control	Jason	99
I Crossed The Line	Kevin Haushultz	100
A Party Gone Wrong	Alicia	102

Section 7
Crystal Meth

Facts about Methamphetamine		104
Confessions of a Meth Addicted Mother	Jennifer Parker	106
Faces 2 Face with Meth	An interview with Sheriff Tom Allman	111
Worth Fighting For	An interview with Crystal Atkinson	115

Section 8
LSD
Facts about LSD		118
A Handful of Candy	Jerilyn Wheeler	119
Living Recklessly	Ashley Warner	120
I Have No Idea How I Got There	Shaun Albertson	122

Section 9
Heroin
Facts about Heroin		126
One Thing Led to Another	Erica Catton	128
Some Kind of Hero?	Savanna Peterson	131
A Crazy Ride	Alicia	133

Section 10
Inhalants
Facts about Inhalants		136
Whippets and Nitrous Oxide Abuse	With quotes from Judy Battle and others	137
No More, Not For Me!	Dillon	139
Confessions of a Teenage Huffer	An interview with Crystal Atkinson	140

Section 11
Ecstasy
Facts about Ecstasy		144
Is This Your Candy?	Savanna Peterson	146
Bombing on Ecstasy	Dillon	147
When the Wonder Fades	An interview with Mikey Rox	149

Section 12
Prescription Drugs
Facts about Prescriptions		158
My Heart Almost Exploded	Brianna	160
Interview with a Pharmacist	Ryan Farmer	163
Overdoing It	An interview with Dez	165
OxyContin: aka Hillbilly Heroin	Rebecca Kanefsky	169

Section 13
Rehab

The Way an Addict Thinks	Scott Gaba, C.A.T.C., C.D.S.	172
Treating Addiction as a Disease	An interview with Dr. Kishore	174
Celebrity Rehab	An interview with Sherry Gaba, LCSW	180
My Rehab Experience	Dillon	183
Treating the Real Problem	Kristen Moeller	187
Treating the Rehab Doctor	Dr. Talia Witkowski	192
Digging My Way Out	Kevin Hauschulz	197
Alateen	Savanna Peterson	199

Section 14
Taking a Stand against Drugs

Times to Be On Guard	Jill Vanderwood	201
What is Expected?	Savanna Peterson	203
Cheerleading	Rebecca Kanefsky	205
I Always Knew	An interview with Actor Tray Chaney	208
Radical Parenting	Vanessa Van Petton	212
Preventive Solutions	Vanessa Van Petton	213
Helping Others	Eryn Gorang	217
Music Keeps Me Focused	Laura Damewood	220
My Path to Success	Devon Green	223
Be a Leader	Dallan Carter	226

A World of Opportunities

See the World	Lina Gassner	231
The Captain of My Life	Debbie Hallamon	232
Seeing the World through a Camera	Georgina	234

Questions for Teens		235
Conclusion: Drugs Make You Un-Smarter	Savanna Peterson	236
Contributors		238
About the Authors		241

"Drug Free Pledge"

I promise to take care of myself.

I promise to make good choices.

I promise to be drug free.

Weldon Hafley Development Center

When I was fourteen I was pressured by my cousin to do drugs. I didn't have a plan in place in case I was ever asked to do drugs, because I never imagined being pressured to do them. I still managed to say no and I never tried them. Rather than drugs, I play basketball, go to drug free parties or do a "Stop the Violence" event.

Keith—age 16, from Philadelphia, PA

When I was sixteen I was offered drugs by my mom, then my friends offered me drugs. You know what they say, "It's the closest people to you who offer it to you." I have tried drugs but don't use now. Rather than drugs, I enjoy bowling and having parties where we dress up and go out to eat.

Kristen—age 18, from SLC, UT

Intro: Be Strong

My name is Savanna Peterson.

I'm fifteen years old and I've lived around drugs my whole life. I live with my mom, an older brother who is nineteen and his girlfriend; a younger sister who is ten and still innocent, and my granddad. I'm strong and I'm keeping away from drugs. I'm trying to become a better person, to be the leader, not the follower. By taking a stand against drugs, I want to become a role model for my younger sister, and have people look up to me.

Doing drugs can change all the good things about you. It's possible to get addicted to something you've only tried once, and your life will be ruined. If that happens, you won't have money, and you'll lose friends and trust with your parents or grandparents. Your little brothers and sisters need someone to look up to who is a good example. It will break their heart to see you becoming someone else. Remember, younger children copy everything you do, and you really don't want to see them doing drugs.

If you are already doing drugs and are having a hard time quitting, go little by little. Stop hanging out with people who talk you into doing it, or spend more time at home, getting to know your family again. Once you get some fresh air and do something fun that doesn't involve drugs, you will see there are better things to do. You will have fun spending your money on something more useful, and unlike drugs, which are gone the minute you take them; you will enjoy a new outfit or an iPod for a very long time.

In this book, I want to show teenagers that doing drugs can seriously ruin their life. You may tell others you're not addicted, but when you feel you're not cool if you don't take a drink, smoke some weed or take a drug, you will know you're addicted. I haven't had experience taking drugs, but I have grown up in a family that does. I get offered drugs and alcohol almost every day, even in my own home, by my brother's friends. I'm not going to lie—I've thought about doing it plenty of times. I decided to make a better choice for my life. I made a commitment never to do drugs. I never used them and I never will, even though a lot of people who know my family tell me, "You're just going through a phase. You're going to sell out in no time." Well, guess what, those people are speaking crap! I will make it. They obviously don't know that I'm nothing like my family! I stay away because I have seen what it does. You may get offered drugs and think, "Well, maybe I should do it once just so they won't bug me about it." I know the first time may not be the last.

If you're involved with drugs, you won't have so much trouble stopping if you stop now. And if you want to try a new drug, it's not worth it. Stop now or you may never stop. The change you make in your life will save trust with your family, help you keep your good friends, and save your time and money. Drugs are just not worth anything. I have seen too many good people go bad.

The age, when kids start doing drugs, is getting younger. There are kids in sixth grade smoking weed with their older brother or sister. They want to try it because they look up to their family member. To a younger kid, a person may look cool and powerful when they do drugs or talk about it, but really, it's the opposite. They are lazy; they have lost the trust of their parents and just a whole lot of negative stuff. Although my brother, mom and cousins smoke weed or take harder drugs, I am drug free and I am my own hero!

Do not give me the excuse that you're around it so much and that you have easy access to drugs and alcohol. Well, guess what? Me too! And I don't do drugs, so don't give me that crap. You can make it. You do not have to follow the footsteps of everyone else; I didn't. Girls like me are a sign of hope that you can walk away from it. It may not be easy and you may be teased every day. Well, I say, "Wow, they're teasing me, but look where their lives are heading. I should be teasing them, but what's the use? I'm the successful one. I'm clean, I know where I'm going, and unlike them, I actually have a life." They're only teasing you because they're jealous that you're drug free. Remember, the person who is teasing you was clean and sober until someone came along and teased them the same exact way they're teasing you. And yeah, they think it's fair to pick on you because someone tricked them into thinking drugs are cool. They were wrong.

We are all cool in our own way!

1. Savanna's Story

☼ Get A Fresh Start ☼

When I came into the World

by Savanna Peterson with Jill Vanderwood

My dad, Troy, was a drug addict, and he was also addicted to taking chances, breaking promises, and lying. He got caught writing bad checks and that's one of the reasons why he went to prison. He always knew how to get his own way because he was good at talking people into things.

When my mom and dad were together, they had a nice house and a nice car, along with a four-wheeler and a trailer to pull it. They started a business selling popular clothes for teenagers called *Modern Teen Outlet*. My dad was a member of the Chamber of Commerce and my parents had their picture taken for the newspaper, cutting the ribbon for the grand opening of the store.

My mom was in heaven with a little son, my brother Brian, a baby girl on the way (me) and a new business that was doing well. My dad was still on parole from prison and he wasn't supposed to leave the state without permission. One week, my parents drove to Texas without permission, and another time, they went on a hunting trip to Idaho with some friends. There were two things wrong with that trip: 1- he was out of state, which is a parole violation and, 2- he was shooting a gun, which is a very bad violation of parole.

The day before I was born, my dad had an appointment with the parole board in the morning and didn't come back. My mom was freaking out. They needed to be at the store, so they could make money to pay the bills.

Later that day, my mom got a call from a federal agency. My dad was being held for parole violations. He had been tracked on his hunting trip to Idaho. Someone had followed them, taking pictures of him out of state and shooting a gun. Some of his checks bounced, so they claimed he was writing bad checks again. They also got him for insurance fraud, because one day my uncle Jason borrowed my dad's blue sports car and totaled it in an accident. Dad put in an insurance claim for the car and spent the money, claiming he had the car repaired. Instead of fixing the car, he took an identical car for a test drive and took pictures of the car to send in to the insurance agency. This fraud was discovered and added to his charges.

My mom was so upset when she heard that my dad had been arrested, she went into labor early and I was born the next day into her unhappy situation.

My dad was in prison, and my mom had a four-year-old and a new baby to take care of. She couldn't keep the store and pay for everything. All she could do was watch as she lost the car, the house, the store, and all the clothes they planned to sell.

We moved into the basement of my grandma's house and lived there until I was eighteen months old. My grandma watched me and my brother while my mom worked at the Butcher Block at Albertson's grocery store. My mom got a storage unit and was able to keep some of her things, like the washer and dryer. She also kept the four-wheeler, but she didn't have a car.

When I was little, my dad would write letters. He sent pictures and presents he made in prison. My dad said he loved me, my mom, and my brother. My brother, who had a different dad, got to go with his dad on the weekends, but I didn't even see my dad. I knew it wasn't fair, and I often wished my brother's dad was my dad. My mom always gave me extra gifts for Christmas and my birthday to make up for my missing father.

I remember the first time I saw my dad, when I was about three years old. I started to cry because he looked scary. He had tattoos and scars like he had been beaten up. When I cried, he got upset and he called me "baby." I'm fifteen and he still calls me "baby."

When I was four, my dad showed up at my birthday party with a bike. That was probably the best birthday party of my life. Dad was out of prison!

My dad never stayed out of prison for longer than about five months before he would get caught breaking parole, crashing his car into a house, embezzling money from his boss, or robbing a bank.

Dad had a nice girl friend who I really liked. She bought me things and took care of me when I would visit. I think she had a drug problem, like my dad, because her teeth were really bad.

Every time my dad got out of prison, he had a new car and an apartment. I'm not sure how he could afford them, but it was probably because he lied.

One time, he almost had my mom believing that he had changed. He told her to move in with him. She was about ready to move all of us into his place when he got picked up again for some stupid scheme. My mom was so glad she didn't move, because we would all have to go through the whole thing again, losing everything and not having a place to live.

☼ **Truth** ☼

My Dad
Savanna Peterson with Grandma Peterson

My dad's birth mother was only thirteen years old when he was born. He was adopted by my grandparents right from the hospital. My Grandma Peterson is a nurse, and she told me that when a girl is very young when she has a baby, most of the nutrition the mother gets while she's pregnant goes to her growing body, rather than the unborn baby. Because his birth mother was still a child, my dad was born with a lot of problems. He had a hard time learning and making decisions. When he was young, a teacher thought he would never read, but he reads very well. He still has a hard time with spelling.

When he was about fourteen, my dad started taking drugs with his adopted brother and some older boys in the neighborhood. Troy has always had the kind of personality where he will do anything to make people like him. Grandma Peterson said, "The younger a person is when they start taking drugs, the harder it is for them ever to get off. Another thing that happens is when they start taking drugs, they stop developing socially. So your dad was acting like a fourteen or sixteen-year-old boy when he was really in his twenties and thirties because he just never developed."

With my dad's drug addiction, he started stealing money from his family and writing bad checks, but the thing that hurt the most was when he stole his mother's wedding ring. The problem became so bad, his parents had to turn him in to the police. These early charges got him involved in the legal system.

My dad has never been violent, but all of his trouble began

when he took his first drugs at age fourteen. All of his prison time was drug-related. One time when he was out on parole, his brother Kevin and a friend stole an ATM machine right off the side of a building. Once they removed the machine, they couldn't load it into their truck. When they realized they were in trouble, they called my dad. Kevin ended up in prison for that, but my dad didn't. Dad swears he didn't know what they were doing. He said he pulled up just before the cops got there.

The next time, he was in trouble. In the middle of the summer he put on a heavy rain coat before walking into a bank. He told the bank teller that he had a gun. They gave him the money while setting off a silent alarm. He nearly got away with it until the dye packs went off. The dye got all over him, on the money, and all over the back seat of his car. The police caught him right away. You can try to wash off the dye, but under a certain light they can still see it. Even if a robber got away with the money, he couldn't spend it because of the dye. My dad went to prison.

Grandma Peterson said, "Everyone has dreams in the beginning of what they want to do in life. Once a person gets a record, they will not be allowed to do certain jobs. The employers do background checks and won't hire convicts. It just destroys their dreams. When their dreams are destroyed, then their whole self-image is gone, and they give up."

My dad is forty-two years old now, and has pretty much ruined his life with drugs and prison.

He is out of prison now and off parole for the first time in my life. Even though he hasn't been caught, he hasn't changed very much. I used to wait for my dad to come and get me when I was a little girl, and to this day, my dad still keeps me waiting. Now, when he says he's coming to pick me up, I say "No, I'm not going," because he's not true to his word. Sometimes Dad will just show up to get me when I'm not expecting him. Last Christmas when I was with him, he stole some tires from a backyard, tried to steal a lady's purse from her car, and smoked weed with his brother and some kids my age while I was in another room on the computer. My grandmother gave me $20 for Christmas. My dad said he'd be back in thirty minutes while he went to the mall to get me an iPod Touch. "Oh, I'm $20 short. Can you loan me the money and I'll pay you back after I go to the bank?" he asked. Well, guess what—my dad never came back with my Christmas gift, and besides that, he stole the money his mother had given me for a gift.

☼ CHOICES ☼

My Mom

by Savanna Peterson with Jill Vanderwood

My mom, Katie, started smoking in the sixth grade. In junior high, she started drinking, smoking weed, and experimenting with drugs.

My mom's parents divorced when she was four years old. She saw her father again when she was six, but didn't even talk to him after that or get a birthday card until she was eighteen.

She was the oldest of four children. She could sometimes be a bossy older sister. She always did her chores and helped her mom clean up until she was in junior high.

It was first noticed in elementary school that she had problems learning things like math and spelling. Other things came easy for her, such as art and P.E.

Mom was adopted by her step-dad when she was eight.

Neither of her parents smoked or drank. When she was in junior high, she really wanted to find her real dad. Since she couldn't find him, she would go home with friends and find a 'cool' dad who liked to party and liked the kind of music kids liked.

Mom was so pretty. She had much older boys interested in her, even when she was in the fifth and sixth grade. She usually had more than one boyfriend. She wanted one who was cute and another one who had money. For Valentine's Day when she was fifteen, she got gifts from more than one guy—a large teddy bear, roses, and balloons. She could talk someone into buying anything she wanted. Her parents wouldn't allow her to date until she was sixteen, but she found a way to do what she wanted. When her mom said she wasn't old enough to go to a concert, she went anyway, having her friends cover for her.

When she was in junior high, her mother would drop her off at the front door of the school and she would go out the back door. My mom started going to truancy court in the eighth grade, after being tardy or absent seventy-three times. The court continued through two years of junior high. My mom and her younger sister spent a lot of time in detention, DT, because of truancy or breaking house arrest. Mom went to school just enough to be a student, but not enough to pass very many of her classes. She stayed in school through the tenth grade, but never made it to eleventh grade.

My brother was born when my mom was eighteen, and she married my brother's dad. She finally went back to high school when she was pregnant with me.

Now that I'm a teenager, guys my age think my mom is hot! She still looks young and really good. No one would think she was a mom with three kids, and my brother is nineteen.

My mom is a single mom with a live-in boy friend. She works nights at a bar to pay bills and provide for her family. Working around liquor, people buy her drinks, but she never drives herself home after drinking. My mom is more like a friend than a mom sometimes.

People Who Have Lived at Our House

My mom is very caring and doesn't have the heart to say no to old friends from her past, her birth father, or my brother's friends. My mom has always let someone live with us, for some odd reason. That is just something I would not do. These people have either lost their homes or got kicked out of their house for drug use. People always come to my mom for help because they see that she made it out of the 'ghetto' apartments where we lived when I was younger. Mom provides a good home for us, but it's hard when so many people eat our food and don't pay rent.

My mom has three kids she has to pay for, and when more and more people come to her for help, it's hard on us kids. Mom loves to help people, but every time she does, they don't appreciate it. I don't think there ever was a time when it was just me, my mom, my brother, and my little sister living in our house. There has always been someone living with us who doesn't pay rent.

☼ REMEMBER WHO YOU ARE ☼

My Brother
by Savanna Peterson

What Was Brian Like When He Was Younger?

When my brother Brian was younger, he liked to dress his own way. When my mom told him he had to wear a certain outfit, he would refuse, and come out with his own style.

When my brother was about three years old, his dad and our mom split up and my brother went with his dad every weekend. He loved seeing his dad, his grandparents, and cousins every week.

When Brian was in kindergarten, he skipped school with a friend and spent the day at the park. The only problem—he didn't know what time it was, so he came home too early. When my mom asked him why he was home, he said he got out of school early. Mom didn't believe him, because none of the other kids in the neighborhood were out of school.

When Brian was in the first grade, Mom took me to the daycare earlier in the day and the bus would pick him up at school, taking him to the same daycare. One day he didn't get on the bus. The daycare called my mom and grandma. Grandma went to the school to look for him. She talked to the teacher and then started looking up and down the street. When she got to our apartment, she found Brian sitting on the outside steps with a group of friends. "Hi, Grandma. Me and my friends are having a party." He was serving them popcorn and water.

"Brian, you were supposed to get on the daycare bus after school. What happened? Did you miss the bus?" Grandma asked.

"No, I didn't want to go there today."

"How did you get into the apartment?"

"I just climbed in the window."

My brother had to take care of me and my little sister a lot. He really did care about us. When Grandma took him to the store, he said, "I want to buy this for Savanna, and I want to buy this for Autumn, and oh, my sister would love that."

Grandma told him he needed to pick out something he liked,

and he said, "If I had a lot of money, I would want to buy things for my sisters."

I Know Brian Cared

I know Brian still cared about my sister and me when he was about twelve, because one day at school he found out about second-hand smoke. My mom smokes and she used to smoke in front of us at home and in the car.

Brian said, "Grandma, smoking can give you cancer."

"I know, Brian. Maybe you can tell your mom to stop smoking."

"She won't! What if we all get cancer? What if Savanna gets cancer or what about Kaitlin?" He didn't worry so much about himself, but he worried about my sister and me. I think he told my mom, because after that, my mom didn't smoke in the house unless she was in her bedroom with the door shut.

Brian's Dad

Brian went with his dad every weekend from the time he was three years old. When Brian was very young, his father was severely burned on a job, working with toxic chemicals. He was given pain pills and became addicted. For years, he lived with his parents and went from job to job. He seemed to be doing much better, had a new job as a hotel manager, and was engaged to a great girl. They were both saving money to buy a mobile home. On several visits to his grandparents' house, everyone would make excuses, telling Brian they didn't know where his dad was. Later, he found out his dad had been in jail. One day, his dad took off with all the money they had saved and no one knew where he was. They found him in jail, and he had spent most of the money on drugs. The next time Brian saw his dad, he showed up at our house with a different girlfriend and nowhere to stay. Brian begged Mom to let his dad stay at the house.

On Brian's birthday, his dad gave him $50. But later that day, the money was missing, and so was his dad. It really hurt my brother when he had to tell Mom to kick his dad and girlfriend out. That was almost three years ago, and he hasn't seen them since. His dad got married and didn't invite my brother. My aunt also saw him at the courthouse, trying to get custody of his new wife's kids. Brian says, "That's messed up, because he doesn't even try to see his own kid."

Getting Away with Things

When Brian was a teenager, he told my grandma he was a kid and he just wanted to see how much he could get away with. He didn't want my grandma to tell my mom. That was when he started painting graffiti on his walls, and then he started skipping school. Mom always said Brian was a kid and she didn't want to take away his creativity. I guess he got away with it.

My brother and his friends began having parties with alcohol, and drugs when my mom was at work. At first, I would clean up the mess after his parties so Mom wouldn't get mad. But then, Mom began telling me to clean up after Brian and his friends because she couldn't get Brian to do it. I finally refused. I usually keep my room clean, unless I have a lot of sunflower seeds or a sleepover. My brother needs to cleanup his own mess.

Drugs Turned My Brother into a Different Person.

- He gave up trust and school
- Let down his family
- Stopped caring about his clothes
- Stopped caring about his looks—dirty hair, didn't shave
- Ruined his teeth because of drugs and doesn't have dental insurance

• He was good-looking, and had a good head on his shoulders—but he didn't finish high school or get a driver's license.
• Drugs took my relationship with my brother and blew it up! He isn't himself anymore.

*My brother and his girlfriend say they've stopped rolling, doing hard drugs, and now they only smoke weed. Brian has never smoked cigarettes. He finally has a job and he's taking better care of himself. Because of all the years when he was partying, we never built a relationship and we still don't get along with each other.

☼ **Be Aware** ☼

Things That Have Disappeared from My House

by Savanna Peterson

Our family has had many things stolen from our house because of drugs. When my brother's friends came over to party, expensive gifts that meant a lot to us began to come up missing. It is very hurtful to have this happen, because we aren't rich and we can't just go out and replace these things. When a person is on drugs, they will do anything to get money. This year, one of my birthday gifts was a deadbolt lock, which I put on my door.

• **4 iPods:** I borrowed my mom's iPod Touch, and someone broke into my room while I was asleep to steal it.
• **X Box 360:** I didn't have a secure lock on my bedroom door, and someone stole the game system. It's really annoying when you have to ask for the same gift the next Christmas, when you would really like to have something else.
• **Computer:** Yes, someone walked right out of the house with the

computer.

- **A TV and stereo:** When I was little, my neighbor knocked on the door to tell the babysitter to go check on the kids outside. When she went out back, someone came in and stole the TV and stereo. By the time my mom got home, the neighbors had time to get it out of their house.
- **3 cell phones**
- **My movie camera:** A friend of our family got me a movie camera for Christmas. I had so many fun movies stored on the disc. When I went to use the camera to film a school dance program, the camera was missing. I have never seen it since.
- **Money:** My mom finally saved enough money to pay rent, and someone stole the money
- **Clothes**
- **Food:** Mom barely had enough money to buy cereal, and she saw a kid walking out of the house with the bags of cereal she had just bought for our breakfast. Even though she caught him, he just kept going.

☼ Change Today ☼

My Dad Taught Me How to Steal
by Savanna Peterson

One time when I went with my dad, I wanted a Three Musketeers candy bar. My dad said he didn't have any money. Then he said, "Oh, just put it in your pocket. I already paid for it."

My dad taught me how to steal! I thought it was so easy. I took my older brother to the store with me when I was about eight and showed him how to steal. From then on, almost every day when we went outside to play, we would go to the store and steal something.

When I was in the sixth grade, I lived near a shopping center. I took two of my friends to the store, and every day we would steal clothes. I went Christmas shoplifting and got the cutest clothes for my mom, brother, little sister, and their friends. It was going well until one of my friends, who was only nine, got caught by her mom. Her mom called both of our moms.

Everyone gets in trouble in a different way. Britney's mom went to the store and paid for the things she stole. Her mom said, "If she wants them that bad, I'll buy them for her." The younger girl's mom took everything back to the stores. At first, my mom was really mad and grounded me, but then she went around telling everyone I had really good taste. She said she would take everything back, until she needed something to wear. She wore a really cute sweater, and then my older brother got into the clothes I'd stolen and gave something to his girlfriend. When my grandma found out about the clothes, she said, "We're going back to the store."

Mom told her they had already worn the clothes, but Grandma said, "Find all the clothes—they have to go back to the store. I won't let Savanna turn out like her dad." She made me figure out which clothes belonged to Kohl's, which belonged to Sears, and which went to Walmart. We got into the car and Grandma drove to my brother's girlfriend's house to get some of the clothes, and then took me back to the store. When I got to Kohl's, the detective already knew about me from the mom who turned us in. They talked to me and warned me not to try it again. I was shaking so bad, I wanted to run out, but I didn't. The detective told me that most families never return any of the stolen items and that I was on record in the store. If I ever did it again, the store would press charges. I would go to court and have to pay a minimum fine of five hundred dollars, even if the value of what I stole was only ten dollars.

Grandma thought I had been punished enough, so she didn't make me go back to Sears or Walmart. She returned the stolen clothes for me. I was scared and embarrassed at the same time.

I did learn my lesson, and I don't even try to steal anything. But I was really mad that Britney got to keep everything!

☼ Informed Choices ☼

What I Believe: Being Straight Edge
by Savanna Peterson

Do you know any teenage boy/girl who has been around drugs their whole life, and still chose to take the other direction? I am going to graduate, go to college, and have a great-paying job. I am also going to go on a lot of trips.

Doing drugs runs in the family, but it stops at me. I hope my little sister will find the right sibling to look up to.

I believe in Jesus Christ, but I'm not a girl who goes to church all the time. I have made a life commitment to be straight edge. A lot of people use straight edge as a trend or to get a boyfriend, but not me. Some kids tell their parents they are straight edge for trust, and then go to raves.

My aunt even thinks that I'm straight edge for that reason.

I have better things to do than waste my life and money on drugs and alcohol. That's just not who I am. It's hard for people to believe that you can be different from the rest. No one thinks I can survive in my family without doing drugs. I've been straight edge for two years now. I know what commitment means and I know how to stick with what I plan to do.

It's hard to make friends with other straight-edge girls because in two weeks or so, they are selling out. They either find out the guy they wanted doesn't like them or they are influenced by people on the outside pointing fingers and saying they aren't going to last a week. They usually do sell out and don't prove anyone wrong. At first, I had people taunting me, but I've proved those people wrong. Once I made the commitment, it wasn't hard at all. I start my own trends and I didn't become straight edge for any guy. People who know me personally know that I stick to my words. I stay away from drugs and out of trouble because I'm doing this for me. Going to raves is a trend in my school. I'm showing people that there are other options.

I am straight edge to stay healthy and try to be as far away from drugs as I can. I've been around drugs and I have always been against them.

XXX--The three X's mean:
    1. Drug-free
    2. Alcohol-free
    3. No promiscuous sex

To others, it's
    1. Drug-free
    2. Tobacco-free
    3. Alcohol-free

But my group includes tobacco along with drugs.
The straight edge themes are:
- "Never Say Die"
- "Fresh Till Death"—because drugs are dirty.

The X symbol first began when underage band members were allowed to play in bars. They were marked with an X on their hand so the bartender wouldn't serve them drinks. In the late 1970's and early 1980's a group of bands and kids were tired of the self-destructive attitude of many bands. They took the X symbol to set themselves apart from members and followers of other punk rock bands. The lyrics written in 1980 by the band Minor Threat suggest that kids:

> Don't need to do cocaine,
> Take speed and pass
> Out at shows
> Because without drugs
> They have the "straight edge."

*lyrics can be found @ straightedge.com

From this song, the movement became known as straight edge. The belief is that drugs and alcohol weren't needed and should be rejected. Straightedge.com * This website represents a strong opposition to drug and alcohol use while using strong language to portray their message.

When I found out what straight edge was, I thought it was a very good idea. A lot of people think it's dumb, but they don't realize how good it is for your life. Many straight edge people are also vegetarian or vegan. Everyone has different thoughts about it. A lot of my old friends have started doing drugs, and that's why I don't have them for friends anymore. When I turned straight edge, I stopped hanging out with my friend I had since the 1st grade because she started smoking weed. I don't even talk to her anymore. My other good friend I had since I was little is in a gang. I pretty much lost all my old friends over my choice to live drug-free, but I gained new friends who have made a commitment, like me. To me, if you turn straight edge, you have to be faithful.

I like to hang out with people older than me. I think most kids my age are too immature. Yeah, I know kids who do drugs. When they ask me, "Savanna, how do you have fun without drugs?" Well, here's my answer. "How did you have fun, before you did drugs? You do not need drugs to have fun! Honestly, I have more fun than most druggies. There are so many fun things you can do in life besides doing XTC or smoking weed every day."

The thing that annoys me the most is when kids at school talk about how crazy their night was when they were rolling. Or they look at something and be like, "Whoa, man, that would be so cool on shrooms!" or "Holy s***, we should do some XTC and look at that, it would be so dank!" No! When people talk like that, I get so annoyed; I want to just pull my hair out! "I'm seriously sorry you don't know how to talk. It was your choice to lose your brain cells from all those drugs." Even when they aren't on drugs, all they talk about is drugs. There are more interesting things in life. I promise you when you quit, it will be the best feeling you will ever have! You will win!

Is straight edge a gang?

To me, straight edge is not a gang, but some people take it too far by slashing tires on beer trucks or waiting around outside a bar to beat people up when they come out. I don't go around with violent people. Straight edge simply means you have the edge because you are straight. My favorite band is *Sleeping Giant*. They even sing about the teachings of Jesus Christ in some of their songs. Because of the straight edge bands, kids are learning to be alert and aware. The bands help kids realize that they are much stronger because they don't deal with their problems by doing drugs. The drug-free message not only comes from school and parents, but it's coming from a cool band. Even though there are still plenty of kids doing drugs, the music and the straight edge message is helping thousands of kids stay away from drugs and stay clean until death. straightedgelifestyle.moonfruit.com

My friends and I like to go to straight edge shows, hang out and listen to straight edge music, talk about stuff, watch movies, and have video game tournaments. Druggies talk about drugs; we talk about other straight edges.

At parties, we play beer pong with orange juice or Kool-Aid. That's a game where you try to get a ping-pong ball into the mug of the opposite team. When you do, the other team drinks the mug.

A lot of parents think that tattoos or piercings lead to drugs. I fully disagree with that. Friends lead kids to drugs. A lot of my straight edge friends who have tattoos and piercings have never taken a drink or drugs.

Straight edge people are like a family to me and help me keep my commitment to be drug free.

☼ **STRENGTH** ☼

The Heroes In My Life
by Savanna Peterson

Grandma Peterson

I don't know how my Grandma Peterson lived through all the problems created by my dad, but she still loves him. She dealt with so much ever since he was a teen—taking drugs and going in and out of prison—and even now, he still acts the same. My grandparents never smoked or drank, and didn't raise their children that way, yet they had two boys who went to prison. Now my grandpa has Alzheimer's disease and he can't even remember her, but she still keeps a smile on her face. In my mind, she is a hero. My Grandma Peterson is a good example of a strong, independent woman. She should get a gold medal for not giving up.

Grandma Vanderwood

My Grandma Vanderwood is my best friend, my hero, and my grandma. She is the most amazing grandma in the world. I trust her more than anyone else in my life. She is the best secret keeper ever, too. She also went through a lot with my mom and aunt who would skip school, do drugs, smoke, and weren't good teenagers. My grandma still wonders how her kids turned out like that. She was a good mom. She doesn't swear, smoke, drink or do drugs.

Aunt Jennifer

My Aunt Jennifer's first husband died when I was one year old. He died on a drug deal, with a bunch of drugs in his car, worth a lot of money. When he got in a car crash, his friend saw he was dead and took all the money and the drugs and took off. This was fourteen years ago, but that affected everyone. My cousin Dillon was hurt by losing his dad. He was so angry, he always used to pick on me—not like *just* pick on me, but push me off chairs. He once picked up his mom's cigarette and burned me really bad on the hand. I still have the scar.

My Aunt Jennifer was hooked on meth for five years. I'm glad my aunt doesn't smoke anymore or do drugs and drink. About ten years ago, she got away from drugs and her old friends, remarried, and started going to church. I am proud of Aunt Jennifer, because her life was bad while she was doing drugs, but she brought herself back up. And you need a lot of strength to do that.

When I was fifteen I felt pressured by my cousins to smoke weed. Then they tried to make me do it. I did try it once, and then I stopped. Since then I started hanging out with kids who don't do drugs and attend the youth group at church. I really don't want to feel the pressure to do things against my will.
Becky—age 18, from SLC, UT

My friends asked me to do drugs. I didn't feel pressured because I just said "No". They knew I didn't want to do it, so they never asked again. Rather than drugs, I like to go shopping; go to movies or eat out.
Michelle—age 16, from Philadelphia, PA

No one has ever asked me to do drugs because I don't believe in that. If they would ever ask me I would say "No", because it's a waste of time and not worth it. I enjoy kicking it at the mall, going to dances and football games with my friends.
Machala—age 15, from SLC, UT

I have had kids at school come up and ask me if I want to buy some drugs or go outside and smoke. I have tried pot and alcohol but I would not recommend this for kids because it's bad for you. Just say no and stick by your word. There are better things out there, like having a real future.
Nicholas—age 18, from SLC, UT

2. How Drugs Affect a Family Personal Stories

How Do Drugs Affect a Family?

How will I know if I have the potential to become an addict if I've never taken drugs?

Look at your family history. Are there smokers, drinkers, or drug addicts in your family? Are there overeaters or under eaters, caffeine abusers, or even people who go to the extreme with anything like religion or exercise?

Cold Turkey
An interview with Brandon

Living With My Mom's Heroin Addiction

- **When did you realize that your parent was on drugs?**

    When I was about six or seven, I started realizing it. My mom and her boyfriend were always sleeping 24/7. I was the only child, but my mom never had time for me. I was on my own at that time between about 5:00 to 10:00 pm. I was also getting myself up every morning, getting ready for school, and catching the bus.
- **Were you getting something to eat?**

    Normally I would just eat at school.

- **Who did you live with?**

    It was just me and my mom and all of her different boyfriends.

    After my stepdad died from an overdose, my mom started doing drugs on the bus while we were going places. On our way to Wendover, Nevada, she would be smoking weed in the front seat and blowing it out the window.

- **Did your mom ever go to work?**

    Sometimes she would go to work, but hardly ever.

- **How was she getting the money for the drugs?**

    We had a doctor who would prescribe us pretty much whatever drug we would ask for. My mom would just turn around and sell it for heroin.

- **Did she have you go to the doctor and get prescriptions?**

    Yes. We both went to doctors to get prescriptions.

- **Did you know why you were doing it?**

    Before that time, it was pretty much her boyfriend supporting her. After he died, I knew that was the only way we could survive. When things got really bad, we would stay with different family members.

- **Did your mom's family know she was on drugs?**

    Yeah, they knew. They'd help us out until they got sick of us and then we'd be on our own. I never had a permanent home, or school. I've lived everywhere in Salt Lake.

- **Were you embarrassed by what was going on in your family?**

    Yes, I was. I could never tell my friends at school, and I had to live a double life. Nobody knew about the drug problems in my family. When they'd ask if my mom had a problem, I'd just deny it every time. I made up glamorous stories about my mom and our travels. I also made sure nobody came to my house.

- **How did your mom finally get clean?**

When I was fifteen, my mom's boyfriend shot her up with a syringe full of heroin and left her for dead in his parents' garage. She fought through it and after that she went through rehab. She withdrew from heroin cold turkey all on her own. It took about a month for her to be able to get out of bed, and take food.

- **Did she go through the withdrawals of heroin cold turkey at the rehab?**

Yes.

- **I'm surprised they didn't give her anything.**

She didn't want anything because she knew that if it was easy for her, she would just go back. She's been on methadone before, trying to get off heroin, but when the methadone was gone, she just went back to heroin. The last time, after the overdose, she went off cold turkey.

- **Where were you while your mom was in rehab?**

She was in detox for two and a half months and during that time, I was pretty much homeless. I had to figure out where to live, what to eat, and how to get to school on my own. I didn't hear from her, and I didn't know if she was dead, or in rehab, or what happened to her. I stayed with different family members most of the time, and finally, one day I heard from my mom.

Mom has been clean for three years now.

☼ Picking up the Pieces ☼

A Tragic Turn of Events
by Elizabeth

My name is Elizabeth. I'm a twenty-eight-year-old PR

professional. In September of 2009, my life took a tragic turn. Michael, my boyfriend of two years, died of a heroin overdose. I never suspected him to be a user—he never showed any of the typical signs—so it came as a complete shock to me, his family, and friends.

It was a sunny Thursday afternoon in Boston and we met up for coffee at a local café. He told me he was going to a business meeting downtown and would be going home later. I knew something was wrong when he wouldn't answer text messages or phone calls. His father and I each filed a missing persons report. Our worst fears were confirmed when Michael was found dead in a hotel room around 8 pm that Friday night.

It's been almost seven months and I still have flashbacks to that day. We had engagement plans for 2010, our life was planned out, and then drugs took over. I don't doubt that he loved me, but he had an addiction that was stronger than any love imaginable.

After Michael's death, I began putting the pieces together to try to understand what went so terribly wrong. From what I know, his father and sister are both recovering alcoholics, but have not abused other substances. One of Michael's friends told me that he dabbled with cocaine when he was about twenty-five. After going to rehab for a few weeks, he continued to drink and apparently was not using drugs. All of his friends kept telling me that I was his angel, that I came into his life at a great time, and he's been clean since meeting me.

Because Michael lived with his family in another town, I rarely saw him during the week. Most weekends were spent with me and we did drink on occasion. I'm not a huge drinker, but enjoy a glass of wine with dinner. A lot of his friends also loved to drink. I'd seen him have his fair share of wild nights, but the two years we were dating, he kept it under control for the most part. During the summer of 2009, we both made a promise not to drink for three entire months. I thought we did it successfully, but did he follow through when I wasn't around? I have no idea.

What he did during the week is now under suspicion. Did he really live at home? Now I wonder if he said he was staying with friends when he was really out of town doing a drug deal.

Michael was in the finance industry, but never seemed to have an actual job. When I met him, he was working for a large corporation in Boston, but was only there for a few months. When we started dating, he was working for a smaller company and quit to start his own business. He later went into business with a former colleague and started doing work for hedge funds. One thing that my family and I always found weird about his situation was that he could never really explain what he did for a living. This "company" he worked for didn't even have a real website. Was it legit?

Michael travelled to New York City about once a month for "business," but now I am almost 100% positive that it was for drug deals. He worked with a very suspicious, older woman. I met her a few times, and she was clearly on some kind of drug at his funeral. Now I wonder if they had an affair, or if she was his drug connection.

My boyfriend lived with his parents, which is a red flag, when you're thirty-two years old, and would often come into Boston for "business deals." He would sometimes crash at my place, and most times he was drunk. When I said I didn't want him strolling in drunk at midnight, he said he would stop drinking at these meetings, but drinking was a huge part of the "business world."

About a month after he passed away, I learned that his mother paid his credit card bills. She either supported his drug habits, or maybe like me, she just didn't know what was going on.

I also found out that Michael borrowed money from friends a lot and would take weekend trips to Vegas alone. I rarely had to pick up a tab when we went out, and he showered me with expensive gifts on my birthday and Christmas. We always took lavish vacations. He absolutely loved Las Vegas and we went there a few times, but we spent all our time together, so I never saw suspicious activity. He did like to gamble and would place bets on sports games and horse races while we were there, but I never thought anything of that.

When I would see him on weekends, he would show up with lottery scratch tickets and say, "This is the big one!" But we'd never win.

We were planning to get engaged in 2010, so we didn't have wedding plans in the works. In the summer of 2009, we were looking at apartments and planned to move in together, but he put that off in July because he wasn't confident he could make rent each month. He then informed me that his father would be able to help out if needed. I didn't want to take that chance, so we decided to hold off on getting the apartment together. After his death, I realized it was a blessing in disguise.

Michael always had over-the-counter medicine like Benadryl and cold pills in his overnight bag. One day, along with his regular remedies, I saw a prescription bottle of Adderall, and he said he had been diagnosed with ADD. He needed the medicine to stay focused and to have the ability to work long hours. When he died, I was able to get my hands on the death certificate, which stated that he died of chronic and acute substance abuse. The exact cause was a heroin overdose. I also learned that Benadryl and Adderall were in his system, along with the heroin.

I always thought of Michael as such a great, kind person,

but this dark cloud over him makes me wonder what else he lied about in our relationship. It's now time to move on and share my story with others. Hopefully it will save lives.

☼ Everything to Gain ☼
I Just Want My Dad Back
by Jessica

My name is Jessica and my father is an alcoholic. Most memories of my father include drinking. I recall him passing out on the floor, urinating in the kitchen trashcan, or my mother trying to help him walk up the steps. Because of his drinking, he missed out on countless softball games and dance recitals. More memories include him shouting and being an angry drunk. One time he lunged at my sister, who was fifteen at the time, and shouted in her face. She was really scared.

Most of my favorite memories begin when I was ten years old. My dad went to rehab and really turned his life around. He channeled his energy into tai chi and focused on traditional father roles, like being a coach in sports and really being involved with our family.

When his brother who was his best friend died, we also lost our dad. He started drinking again after eight years of sobriety. He's been drinking for nine years now. This time, my mother left him. No one wants to visit him because his house is such a mess. Dad gave up his job, so he's not even functioning in society. When he calls, I quickly assess whether he is sober. When my dad is drunk, I tell him I have to go, because I can't make sense out of his drunken conversation.

Now I'm twenty-seven years old and getting married in a year and a half. As every little girl dreams of her wedding day, she wants her dad to walk her down the aisle. But it's different in my case. I tell him I love him and I want him to turn things around, but if he doesn't at least get a job, he can't walk me down the aisle. I want him to stop drinking and to be the person he can be. If he doesn't come to my wedding, or doesn't live long enough to see me get married, it will be his choice. It will mean he chose alcohol once again. He chose to miss out on another great memory he could've had with his kids.

☼ FIGHT FOR YOUR FUTURE ☼

A CASE OF MISTAKEN IDENTITY
Interview with Jason London, Hollywood Actor

• **Jason, it seems very exciting to have a twin brother and even more exciting that you have both made it in Hollywood. Do people often mistake you for Jeremy?**

As twins, it becomes a part of life to be mistaken for each other. It never bothered me when I was growing up. I'm a twin, and I still think seeing two people who look the same is strange and fascinating. It can be a good thing or a bad thing. As adults, there have been times when being mistaken for my brother, who has had some very public drug problems, has been very bad for me. It usually takes a person meeting me to realize that I'm not the one they have read so much about.

• **Did you and your brother always know you would be actors?**

We grew up on farms in Oklahoma. Becoming an actor wasn't even in the realm of possibility. I figured I would become an athlete or a musician before becoming an actor. However, I remember a time when we were about fifteen, and Jeremy asked me if I had a strange feeling we were going to be famous. Although I couldn't imagine why, I definitely had a strong feeling that we would end up in the public eye. There was no real reason for these feelings. But, somehow, we both knew.

- **How did you pursue your acting careers?**

When I was fifteen, I got my foot caught in the lift mechanism of a forklift and two of my toes were cut off. I had to put sports to the side until I healed, so I decided to take drama. Jeremy had also decided to take the same class. We soon discovered that we were pretty talented and began winning awards for it. Our dreams went about as far as getting roles in school productions, perhaps even a commercial some day. But the idea of actually acting in movies seemed as ridiculous as becoming an astronaut. When you grow up so far removed from these worlds, they really do seem that far away.

I had bought a 1965 Mustang with the settlement money from the foot accident. Between the car and my girlfriend, my focus on drama stretched only as far as school activities. It was actually Jeremy who wanted to audition outside of school drama. They were casting a movie in Dallas to be directed by Robert Mulligan, the director of "To Kill a Mockingbird," The movie they were casting was staring a very young Reese Witherspoon, along with a pedigreed cast including Sam Waterson. Jeremy wanted to audition for the lead, but he needed a ride. I had a car, and no real interest in going, but said I'd take him as long as we were back in time for me to go on a date or something like that. It was a huge open call and about 200 people got up and did what I thought wasn't the right take. I finally—really more out of frustration than anything—decided to get up and do it. I ended up booking the part. The movie was "The Man in the Moon," and it was an incredible baptism.

After that, I booked a series called "I'll Fly Away"—also staring Sam Waterson—in Atlanta. I was all set to move, and then the night before I was to leave, my agent called and said, "Unpack your bags. The studio isn't letting you out of the contract. You can't do the series." I had done a pilot that never got picked up the previous year for another network. I was devastated, and so were the producers of "I'll Fly Away." When I spoke with them, I told them I had a twin brother who also wanted to act, and that maybe, if they liked me so much, they should consider him. I told Jeremy exactly what I had done in the audition to book the part. He went in, they ended up casting him, and he moved to Atlanta. That is how we both got started—because of two severed toes.

• **I understand that your brother has taken the hard road of drug abuse, going in and out of rehab. What kind of problems has he had with drugs, and what drugs has he abused?**

Yes, my brother has had (and continues to have) some severe—and very public—problems with addiction, and everything that goes along with that. It's been a long, hard road for the whole family and many of his closest friends. We have gone through a few different addictions with him in the last few years. There was the heroin phase and then the cocaine phase, but they didn't last very long. The main issue with Jeremy has been prescription pills. You name it; he was on it at one point or another. The opiate-based meds were the main problem, however. They are the center of every issue he has. His entire existence has been altered and manipulated by these drugs. One thing I want to make clear is that I don't claim to be an angel. I have had my days of overindulgence. The difference is that I was always horribly afraid of addiction. In

Hollywood, as a young adult, it's almost a rite of passage to party. It's why there is such a high percentage of addiction, arrests, and death. I used to smoke a lot of pot and experiment with a few other things. Luckily, my body cannot handle any kind of hard drug or I may have ended up like my brother and so many other people I know. I became a father at twenty-three. I was a father and a husband and I checked out of the Hollywood scene.

• **How have your brother's addictions affected your life and your career?**

Unfortunately, people mistake me for him quite often, or don't understand that there are two of us. I say "unfortunately" because this is a very small town. People hear "J" and "London" and they immediately go, "No way, we're not going down that road!" That's because they've either already been burned by him or been witness to his illness. Inevitably, someone explains that it's not me, that there are two of us, and that it was most certainly Jeremy about whom they are speaking. But how many people have thought that or made a decision based on that belief? I don't know. I'm sure it has cost me in my career. All I can do is work twice as hard to prove that I am not him. As far as how it's affected my life? It's been a nightmare for my family. It's a hard thing to watch. No matter what one does for an addict and no matter how much love they are shown, until they decide to get help and get better, all the family can do is hope. If you help too much, they never hit bottom. And if they never hit bottom, they don't realize how bad their problems are. If someone is unwilling to admit that there is a problem in the first place, there is nowhere to go. You can't fall out of a basement window. The saddest truth is: you simply cannot help someone who does not want help for himself.

☼ **ENCOURAGE OTHERS** ☼

THE POWER OF FORGIVENESS
by Brooks Gibbs
Teen Motivational Speaker

If you *really* want to change your painful thoughts of hate, you must forgive those who have hurt you. I can't tell you how important this is, but after you've experienced it, you'll understand. "Forgiveness" is another word that is commonly misunderstood. When I talk to teens about forgiveness, they often get squeamish and shy. It sounds too deep, psychological, or religious to them.

It's not that complicated. Forgiveness, simply put, is **releasing the person that did you wrong from the responsibility of fixing it.**

Some young people actually enjoy their anger. They feel that the anger is like a prison in their mind that locks up people they don't like. They are afraid that if they forgive someone completely, it will let that person out of the prison and off the hook. They don't want to see that bully go free. One way or another, addicts will pay the price for their actions. The problem is that refusal to forgive others locks *us* up in our own prison of anger and hate, and we become chained to our pain. It's like drinking poison, hoping your enemy dies—but it ends up killing you. The cool thing is that getting free from the trap of resentment is totally within our control.

Forgiveness is a choice. It is in your power right now to forgive your enemy. You shouldn't wait for the person to apologize or change their behavior—you must forgive them in your heart and mind as soon as possible. I believe that when you allow the addict to stay in your mind through angry thoughts and feelings, the addict is winning and you are losing. It is as if the addict is controlling you from the inside the cell of your mind, keeping you from happiness and stealing your personality. When you forgive, however, all of that is released. The chains of the past fall away and you have the freedom to live and love like never before.

In order to get there, however, you might have to overcome some common misunderstandings about forgiveness:

- Many people feel that if they forgive, they have to forget. They think that if they forgive, they are denying that the painful event ever happened. Not so. You were hurt by someone and I would never expect you to deny that fact.
- Many people feel that if they forgive, they might also forget and be put in the same situation again. Not so. I am not asking you to forgive and forget. I am just asking you to forgive. Remember, we need to live in truth. Truth has a way of making us "street-smart" and keeps us from being hurt the same way twice. When you combine truth with forgiveness, you have an awesome combination. You are able to remember the hurtful event, remember how much it affected you, but then move forward without lingering hatred or anger toward that person. You have forgiven them and are moving on! Living in forgiveness will set you free—living in truth will keep you smart.
- Some people are afraid that if they choose forgiveness, they are basically saying that it was okay that the addict hurt them. This is also wrong. It was not okay, and is never okay for someone to hurt you. It is wrong. Forgiveness doesn't mean you have to approve of the wrongdoing.
- Some people want the addict to come crawling to them, asking for forgiveness before they are willing to grant it. Listen to me very carefully—you can't wait for the person who hurt you to apologize or change their ways. If you wait for them, you will continue to hurt

forever, and the hurt will grow into hate and eventually hijack your happiness forever. Trust me.

• Some people think that they have to confront their enemy face-to-face. The thought of speaking to them turns their stomach. The good news is that you don't have to confront them. Forgiveness is something that you do internally, in your heart and mind. Sometimes it helps to forgive the person face-to-face, but it isn't necessary. Get this—forgiveness is not for them, anyway. It is for you! It frees you from the conflict and empowers you to move on.

Finally, many of us wrestle with this thought: "But they don't deserve forgiveness! They hurt me too badly." Believe me, I understand pain. People can do and say the most hurtful things, and there have been people you have hurt. So please, don't buy into the lie that someone is too bad or too hurtful to deserve forgiveness. The people you have hurt could continue to harbor resentment toward you. That wouldn't be cool, would it? Wouldn't you love to be released from the responsibility to fix what you have done? That's what forgiveness is all about. It's undeserved grace. It's a "get out of jail free" card for the one who deserves to be locked up. It is kindness extended to the addict who doesn't deserve it.

Forgiveness is totally illogical to the human mind, but something in your soul knows that it's the right thing to do, doesn't it? It's going to take incredible courage to lay down your anger once and for all, and choose to forgive. It may be one of the hardest decisions of your life. But let me tell you from my own experience—it will give you your life back. Forgiveness really is a choice. It's not something that happens over time, gradually. Forgiveness only happens by choice at a moment in time. A moment just like *now*. Today. My friend, you are about to have a breakthrough. I can feel it, even as I write this.

Would you be willing to take a leap of faith with me right now? Grab some paper and something to write with, and then write three things:

1. **The Offense.** I want to challenge you right now to write about the pain that has been inflicted on you. Go into as much detail as you need. Let the tears flow.

2. **The Truth.** Write down why this was wrong, and what would have been the right thing for them to do or say.

3. **The Forgiveness.** Then write a short statement of forgiveness to the people who caused the offense. Say their names out loud to yourself and tell them that you release them from the responsibility to fix what they did. Tell them what they said was not true. They were wrong to say what they said and do what they did. Then commit to them that you will no longer harbor angry thoughts about them.

This is how it looked when I wrote about my dad:

The Offense: Dad, you left me when I was young. You caused me so much pain with your alcohol addiction and your inability to be there for me when I needed you.

The Truth: I deserved a father figure who would never leave me or forsake me. You should have been a better example to me. I have learned, from your mistakes, how not to live my life.

Forgive: Dad, I forgive you for hurting me so deeply. There is nothing you can do to fix what you have done, so I release you from my anger. I no longer look to you with hatred. I am in charge of my own life now, and I am moving on. I hope we can have a better relationship now that I am slowly being healed, one day at a time.

So you write the stuff down, and then, let it go. You might want to tear up what you have written as a symbol that you are moving on, or you might want to keep it as a reminder that you are choosing to forgive, even when it doesn't feel right. Either way, never bring it up in your relationship with them or allow your mind to dwell on that pain again. You are uprooting the pain from the deepest part of your heart and casting it away. You might need to talk with a counselor or pastor or maybe even the police about what happened, but you are breaking the anger/hatred cycle and setting your heart free with love.

I am living proof that this stuff works. If you are able to uproot the hatred you feel toward others and really deal with the hurt that is deep within, then you can experience freedom from the bondage of hate. I personally have experienced massive healing from my hurtful past.

I no longer feel any anger toward my dad. I have the most intense love for him, and our relationship now is vibrant. My love led him to desire a clean and sober life. He is now free from addiction, largely because of my effort to treat him with kindness and respect.

I have totally forgiven the bullies who spent years harassing me in school. I don't hold grudges or have any hard feelings toward anyone. That is the truth about me. And guess what? You can experience the same thing! You don't need to hold on to any pain or sadness from your past. You can rise above the hurt, lay down the hatred, and become the loving person you have dreamed about being. When you do this, you are uprooting the pain from the deepest part of your heart and casting it away.

What a powerful opportunity you have right now to change your life through the power of love, forgiveness, and truth.
Do it. Now.

"Don't Let Drugs Disguise You"
Saginaw Elementary, Texas

3. Alcohol

What should you do when someone close to you is drinking too much?

Tell them how you feel. Write it in a letter so they can read it. Be completely honest about what their drinking is doing to them and how it is affecting those around them. Give them an ultimatum: *You either quit drinking, or you lose our friendship. It's your choice. I can't be a silent bystander as you ruin your life.*

Brooks Gibbs
Teen Motivational Speaker

While a patient cannot die from withdrawal of narcotics or stimulants, withdrawal can be highly dangerous and, in the case of alcohol and benzodiazepine abuse, if detoxification is not monitored

carefully by a physician, the patient could die.
Dr. Punyamurtula Kishore
President PMA
President of the National Library of Additions

The dangers of alcohol use in adolescents: Lower body weight increases the danger of over drinking in adolescents. Impairment by alcohol can cause problems such as date rape, serious injuries or saying things you shouldn't say or doing things you wouldn't normally do—such as running in front of a car or removing your clothes outside. These actions can ruin your reputation or even kill you. Binge drinking or overdrinking can cause alcohol poisoning and death. Driving a car under the influence or riding with a driver who says they aren't drunk can kill you, your friends, innocent pedestrians, or others on the road. Underage drinking can ruin your life. It can lead to teenage pregnancy, make you lose your position on a sports team, lose your scholarship to college, or cause a lifetime of alcohol addiction.

Common Myths about sobering up include drinking black coffee, taking a cold bath or shower, sleeping it off, or walking it off. But these are just myths—they don't work. The only thing that reverses the effects of alcohol is time—something you may not have if you are suffering from alcohol poisoning. And many different factors affect the level of intoxication in an individual, so it's difficult to gauge exactly how much is too much.

What Happens to Your Body When You Get Alcohol Poisoning?

Over-drinking can depress the nerves which control the involuntary actions of breathing and the gag reflex (which prevents choking). A fatal dose of alcohol will eventually stop these functions and the person could either stop breathing or choke.

Alcohol irritates the stomach, which also causes vomiting. If an excessive drinker becomes unconscious, there is danger of choking on the vomit.

It's dangerous to assume that an unconscious person will be fine if they sleep it off. A person's blood alcohol concentration (BAC) can continue to rise even while they are passed out. After a person stops drinking, the alcohol in the stomach continues to enter the bloodstream and circulates through the body.

Signs of Alcohol Poisoning

Mental confusion, stupor, coma, or the person cannot be awakened

Vomiting

Seizures

Slow breathing (fewer than 8 breaths per minute)

Irregular breathing (10 seconds or more between breaths)

Hypothermia (low body temperature), bluish skin color or paleness

Information is used with permission from College Drinking Prevention.gov

About Drunk Driving

Geauga County Common Pleas Court Judge Forrest W. Burt sees numerous cases come through his courtroom. Some people think that drinking is a laughing matter.

"The laughter stops at the scene of an accident, or in an emergency room, and most certainly at a funeral home.

"Invariably, I am told that the person before me is not a bad person—it's just that he or she has an illness, or an addiction. The defendant needs treatment, not prison.

"Alcoholism is an illness; drug addiction is a disease. Driving while under the influence is a crime. I almost always tell the person who is being sentenced, 'Your drinking (or your drug use) is not why you're here. You chose to get behind the wheel of a car and go out onto the highway. That was when you began to be a felon.'"

Judge Burt's statements are used with his permission. This article was printed in The News Herald: December 31, 2009

People with normal thinking don't put something in their bodies to feel different. Normal people may take a drink once in a while. If you are a blackout drinker, you cross that line. You will drink to that limit again, hurt yourself, or hurt someone else.
Scott Gaba, C.A.T.C., C.D.S.

☼ **MAINTAIN SOBRIETY** ☼

IT'S ALWAYS GOING TO HAUNT ME
by Dez - age 26

Dez is also the author of *"Over Doing It"* in the Prescription Drugs section.

I've been smoking cigarettes since I was twelve. When I was fourteen, I started smoking weed and drinking.

I still have a serious problem with alcohol. My thing is, I've got to quit my drinking because I make these horrible decisions when I'm wasted on alcohol. That's what makes me want to get high; I lose my inhibition. It's just bad to see—when people are high, it just clouds them so bad.

I'm a late bloomer. I've finally figured out that you can't depress your feelings. A lot of times, I'll wake up and feel bad about myself, about what I'm doing, and then the easiest thing to do is just go get high. Or go get a rush somehow, like stealing. Stealing is just like another drug.

• **Doesn't stealing go along with the drug habit?**

Yes, it does. Oh, by far, and it's easier to get drugs or alcohol by stealing. What I do is I steal alcohol from stores to support my drinking, or trade for whatever drug I want. Alcohol is just as much of a drug as anything else. It's as much of an addiction as drugs, and it's an addiction to a chemical that's making you feel different.

• **Have you been caught stealing?**

Yes, numerous times. For all the times I've been caught stealing, I got away with it hundreds of times. I work in construction. Jobs dry out and then the liquor dries out, and then it's like there's no end in sight, and there are all these excuses I give myself about why I want to drink and the only way I can drink is if I steal something. I am my own worst enemy. I should just listen to myself to see if I really have these needs, and I really don't. I'm unhappy because of my own actions. It makes me baffled. Is my mind that powerful to deceive me?

Actually, I got caught stealing five months ago. I'm supposed to report to jail in three days and I've been sentenced for six months. I'm twenty-six and that's why they want to throw the book at me. I did the crime, I'll do the time. In California they have halftime right now so I'll only serve 90 days. I'm not a violent criminal, really. It's going to help me better myself. I won't be able to smoke, I won't be able to drink, and I can work there. I can get healthy by not having to drink all the time.

County jail is different from prison. I've been there a few times. If I get caught again, I'll be sentenced for two years, but I will only have to serve eight months. That won't be in the county jail. I will have to go to the penitentiary. When I get out this time, I will be sober and I won't steal again.

• **When you went to jail, was it always for stealing?**

Yeah, yeah, I have no drug convictions at all. That's because I never have drugs. They're always gone. I've been really good the last couple of months, especially after I got caught.

• **Did you ever have a DUI, or an accident while under the influence?**

I crashed my car into a wall trying to evade the police.

• **Were you running from the police?**

I ran from the police after stealing alcohol, but I wasn't drunk. I didn't get a DUI—I was charged with theft. I crashed the car, and then ran away. I thought, I've gotta be accountable for this, so I ran back.

• **They already had your car and they knew whose car it was.**

Yeah, it was in my mom's name, so you know, I had to take the rap. I did 120 days and paid a fine. I don't think anyone should take the responsibility for my bad decisions. It's tough to face the results of my poor choices, but it's growing up. I look back and say, wow, this is what I have behind me. I want something better in front of me.

• **Well, it sounds like you're smart and you've really thought it through, so it's time for action.**

I'm just fighting with my addiction, and it's a battle. It's always going to be a battle. It's like, if someone says, "I'm never going to do it again," you can never say that, because there might be a time in your life where you might relapse. Relapse is a part of recovery.

• **Most people have relapsed, but after several tries, many people get sober again and make it.**

It takes a couple times, but it's worth it, if you can be sober.

Can you put a price on that? At first you're going to tell yourself, 'I can never do it again.' But then you're going to want to do it even more. You need to make that choice. What I've found is that you want to make a choice not to surround yourself with those people. If you don't go around people who do drugs, you're not going to do drugs. If you don't go to bars, you're not going to drink.

If I could go back, I would have never tried alcohol or drugs, because now that I know, it's always going to haunt me, for the rest of my life.

☼ Find the Way Back ☼

The Other Side of Alcoholism
by Jill Vanderwood

Surviving a five-year marriage to an alcoholic

At first, I would drink with my husband occasionally, since the only way to spend time with him was in a bar. I soon found that the only way I could handle his drinking was when I was sober. I have since developed an aversion to alcohol. I can't even stand the smell.

I overheard my teenage niece in a conversation with her mother. "Mom, I don't see anything wrong with dating a guy who drinks. It's not like I'm going to marry him!"

I couldn't help stepping in and telling her just what's wrong with that choice.

In high school, my friend apparently had the same conversation with her parents. When I was asked out by her ex-boyfriend, I asked her if she would mind if I dated him. She said, "No, go ahead. My parents don't want me to go out with him because he drinks."

I was not brought up around alcohol, drugs, or tobacco, and had no idea about any of it. My dad did warn us about LSD after he read about a girl who overdosed and sustained brain damage—ending up in a vegetative condition. On many occasions, before we left the house, Dad warned me and my sisters not to let anyone we didn't know give us anything to eat or drink. I had also been warned in school about heroin, but no one talked to me about alcohol.

Bob was the cutest guy I knew, and he paid attention to me. I was very shy, and other than meeting guys at dances and one other boyfriend, I hadn't had much experience with boys. My junior year of high school, I always walked down a certain hallway at school just so I'd run into Bob between classes. Soon we were dating and I couldn't wait for him to call me each day. We often walked home together and went to activities with other friends.

One day, my girlfriends were laughing, but no one wanted to tell me what they were laughing about. After much prodding, one girl who had broken up with Bob giggled, "If you and Bob get married, you will have the cutest kids."

Other girls told me, "If you ever break up with him, let me know."

In high school, Bob beat up a guy for hitting his girlfriend. I also noticed that he told the truth, even if it got him into trouble, and I remember him being very upset with his brother-in-law for cheating on his sister.

I had only dated him for a few months when he quit high school and went into the Army. We wrote letters and talked on the phone, but spent very little time together. I only saw him in person during a few weeks of leave from the Army. During my senior year, when he'd been gone for nearly a year, he came home and gave me an engagement ring.

When his mom told me not to marry him, I just laughed. I knew he was kind of a bad boy, but I liked the sense of adventure.

Looking back, there were signs of problems. He broke into his parents' bedroom to take his mom's Valium pills "so he could sleep." He also broke into their wine cellar and took some wine out of several bottles, and he wouldn't go to a dance before having a drink. When he'd call me from his duty station in the Army, he was usually drunk. On one of his leave visits, he told me he had ulcers and had to be careful what he ate or drank—he could have milk, but avoided orange juice. It never registered in my mind that these behaviors were signs of a problem.

We had dated long distance for almost three years, but marriage was a different thing. The guy I loved showed signs I had never seen before. At first, he drank on weekends—then he was drinking weeknights and wouldn't get up for work. It should have been fun and exciting to be newlyweds, but I sat alone all day in the house, without a phone, and then I sat alone while he went out to drink with his buddies. I didn't work, and he only got paid once a month by the Army. On paydays, he would come home very late at night, and then he would hand me what was left of his paycheck. I had to figure out how to make the money stretch for the rest of the month, with what was left after he treated the whole bar with a drink "on him."

Then there was the abuse. When he was drinking, his temper would go out of control. I often had bruises, a fat lip, or a black eye. He would blame the abuse on me, for being upset with him. I was young, pregnant, and hundreds of miles away from my family.

On weekends, Bob and his friends would party in our house

with drugs, alcohol, and pot. Often someone would come over and offer him a new drug—once, they brought a horse tranquilizer. They would all be laughing and acting silly while I sat alone in our bedroom, turning up the volume on the TV to drown out the noise.

After Bob was discharged from the Army, we moved back east to live with my family. He got my younger siblings hooked on marijuana. I was then expecting my second child. Bob worked for a landscaping company until he got hired by a factory that made paper cartons, such as Coke and Pepsi bottle holders. He was making above minimum wage and we were living better.

When we were in our own home again, he loved finding people who drank as much as he did. I endured weekends with him in the drunk tank, or having neighbors bring him home after finding him passed out in their yards. Even though I had the care of two young children, I felt responsible for and embarrassed by his misdeeds. And, at home, the abuse continued. In addition to the support of my family, I joined a church, which also gave me support.

During my third pregnancy, my husband quit his job, leaving me with no way to pay for the birth of our son. I put my two young daughters in the stroller and walked several miles to the office of his former company. I was very pregnant and marched in to persuade them not to cancel our insurance. It was agreed that if I would pay $100, they would cover the birth of our child.

Bob contacted a buddy from the Army to help him find a job at the telephone company. Just before the baby was due, he traveled with our oldest daughter to Colorado on a Greyhound bus. That job fell through, and he had to pay a babysitter so he could work in a tire store. I needed to find a way to get to Colorado with a new baby and a one-and-a-half year old. If he hadn't taken our daughter, I wouldn't have made the trip, and he knew it. My church paid for my airline ticket.

We found an apartment, and I located a branch of my church right away. Bob did pretty well working in the tire store until he showed up late too many times. We had no furniture, no car, and just our clothing, dishes, bedding, and towels, along with a borrowed washing machine. My mother was extremely worried about our move, but thankfully, we had a new church family in Colorado.

I really thought that by moving to another state, away from his druggie friends, we could have a fresh start. I was wrong. Within a short period of time, he had the same group of friends—only their names and faces were different. He knew how to get hold of any substance he wanted, and the problems only followed.

I had WIC to help provide food for the baby and my two young daughters. I also applied for government welfare to help support us when he lost his job. Finally, he got another job at Winchell's Donuts for minimum wage. I was put into the situation of deciding whether to buy food stamps or pay rent. This made it necessary for all of us to eat the food provided by the WIC coupons. We had cheese, eggs, milk, juice, and cereal, and we came up with enough money to buy bread, peanut butter, and jam.

There were two things I would never allow. First, I wouldn't allow my husband to buy a car. He could have purchased one with our tax returns, but I thought he'd kill us all by driving drunk, so I would always make sure the money was spent on other things. Secondly, I would never allow him to sell drugs. We had a neighbor who had been put in prison for selling when her baby was only a few months old. When I met her, she had just gotten out of prison and had not been able to be a mother to her little girl until she was three years old. No matter how poorly we were living, when my husband wanted to sell marijuana from our home, I would not allow it.

One snowy December night, while other people were putting up Christmas trees and wrapping gifts for their families, I was forced to leave my husband in order to protect my children from their raging father. Members of my church took me and the children into their home until we could relocate, and didn't let my husband know where we were living. He gave us our clothes, but he wouldn't even give me the kids' birth certificates. He thought we would come back if he didn't give us anything, but I didn't care if I lost everything.

With help from my church, we found an apartment and started a new life. The church paid our rent and provided food. I babysat, ironed, and sewed for other people to pay for clothing and other bills.

I went to counseling for several years to deal with the effects of my husband's alcoholism and abuse. Many women either go back to the abuser, or marry someone just like the one they left. Not me. I was a single mother for four years.

When I was looking for a new husband, God led me to a man who was the complete opposite. The man I married doesn't drink, smoke, or do drugs. My current husband will work for the same company until he retires, rather than hopping from job to job.

In our new life, I have never wondered how I was going to feed or clothe my children. I put myself through school so I could support my family on my own, if needed.

Signs of Alcoholism
by Jill Vanderwood

If you don't think there is any harm in dating a guy or girl who drinks, look for the signs.
• Does he have a drink before he goes to a dance?

- Does he ever drink on a weeknight when he needs to work or go to school the next day?
- Does he miss work or school because he drank too much?
- Does he steal drinks from his parents' wine cellar or liquor cabinet?
- Do all dates involve alcohol or other substances?
- Does he sound drunk when he calls you on the phone?
- Does he drink too much and pass out?
- Does he enjoy finding others who can drink as much as he does?
- Does he seem fun, the life of the party—after a few drinks?
- Does he give money to an older friend to buy alcohol?
- Notice how often your boyfriend/girlfriend drinks in a week.
- Notice how many drinks he/she has in one night.
- Does he say things like—"I know the perfect cure for a hangover? Start drinking again!"
- Does he say things like—"I know the perfect cure for that"? Whether it's a cold, the flu, or a tummy ache, he will say the perfect cure for what ails you is a drink.
- Does he use prescription drugs prescribed to someone else?
- Does he use or talk about using marijuana—pot or weed?
- Does he say "It's just pot, and pot should be legal anyway"?
- Does he talk about drugs and alcohol a lot, like, "I know where we can get some good weed," or "I know where we can party with no parents"?
- Does he try to get you to use these substances?
- Does he have money that isn't accounted for—which could come from selling drugs?

If you said yes to any of these questions, your boy/girlfriend is likely to have a drug or alcohol problem.

What should I do if I've been drinking?
by Jill Vanderwood

Call for a ride, even if you have your parent's car.

If you drive under the influence of drugs or alcohol:

You might make it home but...

1. You could get pulled over
2. The car could be impounded
3. You will have a DUI on your record
4. You could have your driving privileges revoked
5. You could wreck your parents car
6. You could wreck other peoples cars
7. You could even kill someone
8. You could get arrested and be tried as an adult
9. You could go to prison for manslaughter.

Which risk are you willing to take? Being grounded or being put into prison? It's your choice.

4. Marijuana

Should you ever supply drinks to an alcoholic? Should you give a drug to an addict, or cigarettes to a smoker?
  No! That is called enabling. If it's easy for an addiction to keep going, there will be no need for the addict to quit.
What is enabling?
  It is anything from supplying the drug to making excuses for the addict. Anything that makes it easy for the addiction to continue falls into the category of enabling. If the addicted person can't easily get the drug, and they are forced to face their problem, they are more likely to quit. So your help, or enabling, may actually allow the

addiction to continue longer.

Facts about Marijuana

In some states, marijuana is legal for medical use. This is a drug that many people might share by taking a drag from a marijuana cigarette and passing it to the next person.

This drug looks like dried parsley and may include stems and seeds. It will be green, brown, or gray. This is often called a gateway drug because it can lead to the use of other, stronger drugs.

Common Names: pot, weed, blunts, chronic, grass, reefer, herb, ganja

How is it Used? Marijuana is usually smoked. It's rolled in papers like a cigarette, called a joint, or in a hollowed-out cigar called a blunt. It is also smoked in pipes, called bowls, or water pipes, called bongs. Sometimes marijuana is mixed in food or brewed like tea.

Effects and Dangers
- Mood swings from happy to depressed
- Causes increased drowsiness
- Elevates heart rate and blood pressure
- Causes red eyes
- Tough on lungs, like a cigarette
- Steady smokers suffer coughs, wheezing, and frequent colds

This drug causes psychological dependency. A teen may use it to feel good or handle stress. Their bodies may demand more and more of this drug to achieve the same effect. Marijuana use can make a person 'laid back' without a care, which causes laziness and will affect job and school performance.

Information from teensdrugabuse.gov

***Using marijuana definitely opened me up to using other drugs.*
Erica**

☼ Accept Help ☼

Mentally Obsessed
by Tina

When I was in high school, I started getting drunk and getting high on the weekends. As the years progressed, my using increased and I tried other drugs, including ecstasy, painkillers, mushrooms, and LSD. By my junior year in high school, I was using drugs as often as I could, but I didn't always have the money to get them. My group of friends definitely changed as my drug use escalated.

The next year, I was using daily. Up until then, I had been a gifted/talented student with good grades and involved in many extracurricular activities. When I got to my senior year, though, drug use and my boyfriend (who I used with) became my top priorities. I quit my activities (cheerleading, choir, etc) and I began showing up late for school or skipping the whole day. My peer group changed dramatically and I began hanging out with 'lower quality' people, who also made drugs number one in their lives.

My parents are adult children of alcoholics and were very aware of the road I was taking. They were strict with me. I did whatever it took to get my drugs and do what I wanted. I ran away, stole from family members, climbed out the window at night—it didn't matter. I did smoke pot at home sometimes, and would cover it up with fragrance. I always had Visine in my eyes, but it really didn't help—it was pretty obvious that I was getting high, and it was hard to hide, but I didn't care. Finally, I gave up the façade.

For awhile, I tried to maintain many different friends and images. I still had my smart, school-oriented friends, and they had only a slight idea of what I was up to. The friends I'd known for a long time were only interested in drinking, and maybe pot, but not harder drugs. As my life went downhill, I seemed to gravitate toward people who did harder drugs.

I knew I had a problem, but with my dedication to my boyfriend, who was a hardcore alcoholic, I really had no hope for change. By this time, I was miserable, but I had alienated everyone I had ever been close to, especially my parents. After being arrested for stealing, I went through one round of outpatient treatment. I was also exposed to Narcotics Anonymous, NA, but didn't take it seriously.

I finally got clean when my parents sent me to a 3-month program in the Alldredge Wilderness Journey Program in West Virginia (sadly, they closed their doors at the end of 2008 due to the economy). This treatment changed my life and I don't think I could have gotten clean at that point without it. I came home from the program in June, wanting a new way of life, but in my heart I wasn't totally committed to doing what it would take to stay clean. My plan was to never do drugs again, but I thought I could just do "controlled drinking" when I got to college.

Once again, I went to a few NA meetings, but decided it was not for me. Shortly thereafter, I began drinking and went on a two-week binge that was a terrifying reality check. I got clean on July 23rd, 2003, and have been clean ever since. I immediately got involved in NA. I got a sponsor, went to meetings every day, and began working the 12 steps. My life changed quickly and I have never looked back! I am still very involved in NA and AA. I go to meetings regularly, use a sponsor, continue working the steps, and do service work. It is a huge part of my life and a great source of joy, happiness, and fellowship.

For me pot was a gateway drug, mainly because of the people I hung out with and what they were doing. I thought that it was "just pot," and how could it be that big of a deal? At some point, it was no longer strong enough for me—I couldn't get high enough to escape my feelings or my life.

I do think marijuana is a problem for kids. It made my brain fuzzy and changed my personality. It creates an altered state. I think it's weird for anyone, especially adults, to use any sort of illegal drugs. I didn't feel that way back then, but today, I wonder *why would you ever desire to do that if you are a well-adjusted person*? Not from a place of judgment, but just the simple fact that it doesn't make sense to use drugs if you like yourself and are happy with your life...and value not doing things that are illegal or dangerous.

I can say from my own experience that marijuana is highly addictive. I had withdrawal when I didn't have it in my system (anger, anxiety, irritability—physical symptoms). I was mentally obsessed with it. It was the center of my life. I would do *anything* to get it (steal, lie, cheat, and more). From being in NA and knowing countless other addicts, my behavior was no different from that of people who were addicted to heroin or cocaine.

I learned in recovery that I have special biochemistry that makes me susceptible to all forms of addiction—alcohol, drugs, exercise, eating disorders, sugar, caffeine—it doesn't matter. I am sensitive to any chemical that can physically alter my brain. There are definitely indicators for addiction, and knowing what I know today, I would spot it in my child. My parents saw it in me. I just was not interested in taking their advice. And that's the thing about addiction—you can't make the addict want to be clean, or want a different way of life. It's something they absolutely must desire for themselves.

☼ **BUILD ON YOUR STRENGTHS** ☼

Just Pot?
Ryan Frazier's Story

We often hear the phrase, "It's just pot," but have you ever thought about what a marijuana charge on your record can do to a career?

This really hit home for thirty-four-year-old Ryan Frazier from Utah. Ryan's dreams nearly shattered when he was charged with possession of marijuana, a misdemeanor with a sentence of between six months and one year in prison and between $1000 and $2500 in fines. Paraphernalia can be as simple as the container used to carry the substance, like a plastic bag. In Utah, a paraphernalia charge can also carry a six-month jail sentence and an additional $1000 fine.

Frazier had a dream of becoming a plumber. Marriage and family came first, making it necessary for him to put aside dreams of an education to take jobs in restaurants and construction to support his family. Six years ago, he was injured in a car accident and unable to continue in a job requiring heavy lifting. He decided it was time for a career change and began his long journey back to school, beginning with his high school diploma. He then pursued his training as a plumber. Working full-time in his chosen trade, attending night school and studying hard, he made his way through the apprenticeship program.

With all the stress of his work and school, Frazier smoked

pot to relax and get to sleep. Several of the small businesses he worked for closed during hard economic times, and he had no record of the apprenticeship hours he had earned. He still needed more hours so he could become a journeyman. "When I finally had enough hours, my company required me to commute out of town, with no reimbursement for lodging or travel expenses. In a small Utah town, I found an inexpensive motel so I could stay during the week and commute home on weekends. After three weeks, the nightmare began.

"I was visiting with a couple guys who also had rooms in the motel. While practicing cords on a guitar, we had a couple of beers. At around 9:30 or 10:00 on a weeknight, someone in the motel must have complained about the noise. We found the outside of our room surrounded by cops. They told us to come out while they searched the room. I was handcuffed, but told I wasn't being arrested, only detained. Before I was searched, they asked me if I had any drugs or sharp objects on my person. I had tools of my trade and a small amount of pot, about the size of a dime. Still leaving me under the impression that I was not being arrested, I was taken to jail.

"I spent two days in jail with one phone call—to my journeyman who was in charge of the job, to tell him I couldn't make it to work. I spent one night on the cold cement floor, with only a wool blanket. The heat would pour in and I would sweat. Then the air conditioner would click on and I would huddle under the scratchy blanket."

Not having his cell phone, Frazier didn't even have a phone number to call his family. Although he called the house phone, no one was home when he called. It seemed hopeless. He worried that without paying rent, his motel room would be padlocked, his expensive tools lost, and his truck impounded. Ryan Frazier had plenty of time to think about pot and the reason he was in jail. Was it "just pot?" Was it worth losing everything he worked so long and hard to achieve?

After three days, Frazier got hold of a bail bondsman, who got him out of jail. He hired a lawyer and called the owner of the company. Even though he called work, he was let go for being a "no show" just because he didn't call the 'big boss' sooner. His truck was put up for collateral in case he didn't show up for court, and he had to take $1500 out of his savings to pay a lawyer.

Ryan Frazier had his hair cut and quit smoking pot. He began attending Narcotics Anonymous meetings and felt great knowing he could pass any drug test. For the first time in many years, he was clean. After three months he was finally able to find work in his trade.

Frazier went to court, four months later, with evidence of passing a drug test, a signed paper from NA, and a good job as a plumber. His lawyer asked for an order of abeyance. For this to be in effect he pled guilty to a marijuana and paraphernalia charge. He was given fifteen more days in jail, which can be served on weekends. If he stayed clean with no further charges for eighteen months, these offences would be removed from his record. It also meant that if he was ever pulled over for a traffic violation, he could be searched and ordered to take a drug test.

Ryan said, "When you go to sleep after smoking pot, you never dream. You never have to face your problems, and forget what it's like to feel emotions. I will never think the same way about pot as I used to. To me, pot is a dream killer."

☼ **CLIMB THE MOUNTAIN** ☼

When I Grow Up
by Jennifer Parker

Jennifer is also the author of "Confessions of a Meth Addicted Mother" in the Meth section.

I married Jason when I was only seventeen. Jason worked with his dad doing construction and we were able to move into our own apartment before our son Dillon was born. That's when Jason discovered a new occupation. He sold marijuana to kids in the area. Kids brought items to him in trade for pot. Soon our home had extra TVs and stereos, which he could sell to buy more marijuana. At times, Jason's newly acquired wealth would go to his head. One friend recalls him standing up on our dining room table with fists full of money, saying, "I'm the man! Look at all this money."

We had a son and a daughter and our family moved at least once a year. We were evicted from one apartment because we didn't pay rent. Jason's main drug dealer paid the bill for us to stay in the best hotels in Salt Lake City. We stayed in the Little America Hotel, ordering room service, and then moved to the Radisson and other luxury suites around the valley. This high living continued for about two months before we found a house to move into.

In our new house, Jason developed an addiction to cocaine and went on binges. He would take off for several days without even calling. When he came home, he seemed pretty normal for awhile. The drug dealing continued, with people making short stops to our house. Four or five other friends lived in our basement and partied night and day.

One day, Jason drove home in a shiny red Cadillac with a white top. He often bragged that this flashy car was a drug dealer's car.

There was usually a bong, which is a tall glass water pipe, set up on our kitchen table for friends to gather and smoke pot. When my mom came to the house, our three-year-old son was playing with the bong. He said, "Grandma, this is for big people to smoke drugs. When I'm big, I'm going to smoke drugs." My mom told him big people don't always smoke drugs. Dillon also pointed out the strong box on the counter, saying, "This is my dad's drug dealer."

One night when there were several of our friends sitting around our house drinking and kids playing around our feet, the police showed up with a warrant. All adults in the home were told to get down on the floor. Jason and I were handcuffed. The kids were taken into the bedroom, where they were scared and crying for Mommy. I was also crying, wanting to go to my kids. Jason talked the police out of taking me to jail by saying he was the only one involved and I didn't know anything about it. He finally convinced them to leave me so I could take care of my two young children. The other people, including my sister, her boyfriend, and my brother were all released, and we watched while drugs were removed from our home and my husband was taken to jail. His shiny red Cadillac was impounded, because it was bought with drug money.

Not long after this arrest, Jason was released, awaiting his sentence. He decided to take an out-of-state trip to deliver several pounds of marijuana. After the arrest, with his Cadillac still in the impound lot, I thought it was too risky for him to take this trip. Jason assured me it would be fine and this would be his last trip. He said he would make a lot of money, and be back in a few days. Jason drove a car with the pot and his friend drove another car with the money. I stayed home waiting and worrying.

I was at the Laundromat when his friend called. Since I was gone, he left a message with my brother, saying there had been an accident. I was in a panic, worried about the accident and not being able to get hold of his friend. I knew they weren't in the car together, but if his friend wasn't hurt, maybe Jason was okay too. Then I thought, if he's okay, he would be calling instead of his friend. I couldn't imagine what had happened. When I finally got the call, I was told that my husband didn't make it. They had just stopped to get something to eat, so I figure he was eating and had been distracted. He hit a truck parked along the side of the road that was loaded with cement barriers. Because of the cement, the truck was weighted down and didn't give at all. It's kind of like hitting a brick wall. Jason wasn't wearing a seatbelt and was thrown out through the sunroof of the car. He was only twenty-four and left behind a wife and two kids. I was only twenty-two and I was a widow. We were finally able to get the Cadillac out of impound, and the charges against Jason had to be dropped. I couldn't explain what happened, to my two-and four-year-old children, so I just said, "Daddy is in the hospital." My mom had to explain that their dad was in heaven and he wouldn't be coming back.

The funeral home wouldn't let anyone help me pick out the casket or the burial plot, even though my father-in-law was paying for everything. I had to run out of the room several times, with tears running out down my face, but when I came back, everyone was just waiting for me to continue. I even wrote the obituary.

After Jason's funeral, a woman who had been friends with Jason since he was a child told me, "When we were kids and talked about what we wanted to be when we grew up, Jason always said he wanted to be a drug dealer."

One day I was in the park away from my older cousins when some teenagers came up to me and offered me some marijuana. They told me to try it and that it would make me feel happy.

It was hard for me to say "No" but then I remembered all the things I was taught at school, so I stayed strong. I told my older cousins that I said "No" and they were proud of me.
Kaylee—age 12: sixth grader from SLC, UT

My brother tried to get me to do drugs. I had no idea that he was doing drugs before that. The drug he offered me was something to smoke.

- Sometimes it's much harder to avoid a problem when it's right in your own home. Do you feel that you can talk to someone about this? If you can't talk to your parents, can you tell another grownup?

Yes, it's harder when it's my own brother. I did talk to a grownup and they talked to him about it. He never asked me again.
Kelsay--age 11: sixth grader from SLC, UT

When I was younger a friend offered me a cigarette. It was really hard to say "No" to a friend. I told him, "No, because it can kill you or make a hole in your throat."

I talked to my parents about this and also told a teacher at school. Rather than smoking or doing drugs, I love to play soccer with my sister and my dad.
Cesar—age 11 : sixth grader from SLC, UT

5. CRACK

WHAT ARE THE SIGNS OF DRUG ADDICTION?
by Brooks Gibbs
Teen Motivational Speaker

• The addict will have built up a drug tolerance. They need to use more of the drug to experience the same effects they used to get with smaller amounts.

• They will take drugs to avoid or relieve withdrawal symptoms. If they go too long without drugs, they experience symptoms such as nausea, restlessness, insomnia, depression, sweating, shaking, and anxiety. They have to take drugs just to feel normal again.

• They will lose control over their drug use. The whole idea of being "under the influence" means that they are under the *control* of a drug. This leads them to do drugs more often, even though they told themselves they wouldn't. They may want to stop using, but they feel powerless.

• Their life revolves around drug use. They spend a lot of time using and thinking about drugs, figuring out how to get them, and recovering from the drug's effects.

• They might abandon activities they used to enjoy, such as hobbies, sports, and socializing, because of the drug use.

• They continue to use drugs, despite knowing it's hurting them. It's causing major problems in their life—blackouts, infections, mood swings, depression, paranoia—but they use anyway.

Facts about Crack Cocaine

Crack is the crystal form of cocaine. It is sold in solid blocks or crystals in colors from yellow to pale pink or white.

Crack is heated and smoked. Its name comes from the cracking or popping sound which comes from heating this substance.

Crack is the most potent form of cocaine. It is also the riskiest. This drug is between 75 to 100% pure and far stronger than the powder form of cocaine.

By smoking crack, the user gets a quicker, more intense high which only lasts about 15 minutes. Addiction can develop rapidly when a drug is smoked—therefore, the user can become an addict after the first time smoking crack.

Cocaine is considered a rich man's drug. On the other hand, crack is so inexpensive, even teens can afford it. As the addiction goes up, so does the price of crack. The dealer knows the addict will pay whatever it takes to satisfy their addiction.

Most common names for crack cocaine: *Notice how many common or food names are used here*

24-7	Electric Kool-Aid	Badrock
Base	Gravel	Rocks
Grit	Rock star	Candy Rox/Roxanne
Hard ball	Scrabble	French Fries
Hard rock	Raw	Snow cake
Cookies	Hot cakes	Sugar block
Crack	Ice cube	Tornado
Crumbs	Jelly beans	Devil drug
Crunch & munch	Kryptonite	Nuggets

Why is Crack so Addictive?

When it comes to psychological dependence, crack cocaine is one of the most powerful drugs. This drug stimulates the pleasure sensors in the brain, which gives a sense of euphoria. The user is very soon addicted to crack and needs to use more and more to reach the same high.

While you're doing crack, you're instantly hooked, immediately. I don't think you quit doing it until it's gone, completely. It's the kind of jones (craving) when you take a hit of crack that you want it so bad, you'll cry for it. That's how bad you want it, that you would actually cry.
Jennifer Parker

Effects of Crack

The intense high is shortly followed by the opposite—extreme depression. Those who use crack can experience rapid heart rate, muscle spasms, and convulsions. The drug can make the user anxious, paranoid and angry, even when they aren't high.

No matter how much of the drug is used or how often, the user is at increased risk of heart attack, stroke, seizure or respiratory failure. All of these can cause sudden death. Information used with permission from Foundation for a Drug-Free World

☼ You Will Make It ☼

I Was Addicted Before I Inhaled My First Hit
by Jennifer Storm

Author of "The Blackout Girl" and "Leave the Light On"

Once I healed from abuse, I didn't have a need to pick up a drink or drugs.

Hanging around with older kids in my neighborhood, I started smoking cigarettes when I was eleven. I have always considered cigarettes to be a drug. At the age of twelve, I was raped by a twenty-eight-year-old man and didn't know how to deal with it. I was very young and learned about sex in a very harsh, abusive environment. To bury my hurt and shame, I began smoking pot. That led to the downward spiral into addiction.

At fifteen, I took LSD and started snorting cocaine. When I was seventeen, I began smoking crack cocaine. Cocaine was always my drug of choice, but I never did any drug without drinking first.

My parents, and pretty much anyone who was around me, knew I had a problem. I skipped school and had to take summer school because I failed three grades. Many people knew how addicted I was and tried to reach me. But I was beyond anyone's reach at that time in my life. My parents put me in therapy, but rape was at the root of all my problems, and at that young age, I was not open, able, or ready to talk about it. The traditional therapy modalities do not really work well with child rape survivors, so it wasn't helpful for me.

During the time I used drugs, I always lived with my family. I supported my $60 to $100-a-day drug habit by stealing money from lockers at school or from my parents. One time, a friend and I got caught stealing from purses at school. We were sent for a drug evaluation, which was followed by a brief probation.

Once I'd picked up on a drug, I would stay with it all day long until I passed out at a boyfriend's house or wherever I was hanging out that day. I tried to maintain jobs, but with serious drug use, that becomes impossible, when all you can think about is the drug.

In order to get me to try crack cocaine, I was told the *big lie*. "This will make all your worries go away. You won't have to feel anything or deal with anything in your life." That was just what I wanted to hear. I didn't want to feel any hurt, emotions, or deal with any of my problems. In my book, *The Blackout Girl*, I make the statement: "I was addicted before I inhaled my first hit." Sure, the drug may cover things up for awhile. When you come down, you have to deal with the fact that you missed school again, all your money is gone, and you have let everyone around you down. On top of that, you have a serious drug problem—so you will only do the whole thing again.

This cycle continued for several years. I ended up in the hospital when I was twenty-one after I tried to kill myself. I woke up and realized *I didn't want to die!* I took any suggestions the doctors were willing to give me. It's a miracle that I'm alive. If I hadn't changed my life, I believe 100% that I would be dead. I haven't picked up drugs or alcohol since, because I knew if I ever used again, I wouldn't make it.

Abuse was the foundation for why I used drugs, and once I healed from abuse, I didn't have a need to pick up a drink or drugs. Drugs don't have to be an option. There are so many other ways that you can learn how to deal with your problems.

Now, I know: there is nothing in this world I can go through which won't be made worse by using drugs.

☼ Accept Your Limitations ☼

Disneyland
by Rebecca Kanefsky

Rebecca is also the author of "The Coke Man", "OxyContin—AKA Hillbilly Heroin" and "Cheerleading".

I spent the first ten years of my life in southern California. Both of my parents are drug addicts, and they separated when I was very young.

My dad and I had a tradition. For every birthday, he would take me to Disneyland. On a weekend visit with my dad, when I was eight and a half, he woke me up early one morning.

"Do you want to go to Disneyland?" he asked, holding my two-year-old brother in his arms.

"Yes!" Even though it wasn't my birthday, I was going to Disneyland! I was so excited, I could barely get ready. I even tried to go in my pajamas, afraid that if I wasn't ready in time, plans would somehow change.

We stopped at my step-grandmother's house to pick up my

step-mom's younger sister, Cecilia, who was twelve, for her first trip to Disneyland. She was so excited, she was crying, and we hadn't even left her house yet.

We drove what seemed an eternity until finally my dad pointed out the Disney castle from the freeway.

"Look, kids, it's Disneyland, and there's the castle!"

All three of us kids were jumping up and down in our seats, making the car rock. Cecilia started crying all over again. I was so excited, I also started crying, and my little brother was so confused, he cried too. My dad was laughing and assuring us, we were going to Disneyland.

He told us we needed to eat at McDonald's before we went into the park. "Food costs an arm and a leg in there. We'll all get Happy Meals." The cheers and happy tears were back on.

We parked right across from Disneyland, at McDonald's. He popped the hood of the car, and let the air out of one tire. Then he taught Cecilia and me how to "hit people up." Cecilia refused and began crying uncontrollably.

"Where's my Happy Meal?" she asked between her now unhappy sobs.

"Go take Michael to the play yard and wait until I get the food," he said.

The first man I asked for money handed me $10.00 on his way into the restaurant and talked with my dad. When he came out, he had more than enough food for all of us. My dad was so proud of me.

He asked me, "You really want to go to Disneyland, don't you?"

"Yes, Daddy," I said, grinning ear to ear. I could tell he was proud of me by the smile on his face, so I eagerly awaited the next person, telling the sad story of our trip to Disneyland being cut short by our broken-down car. This was followed by the next one, and the next one, and so on.

It was early when we got to McDonald's, and after a few hours, the fun had worn off. I was growing anxious, my brother and my dad had fallen asleep in the backseat of the car, and Cecilia sat in the front seat, still crying. When my dad finally woke up, I handed him all the money I had hustled.

"Okay, now we're off," he said. I was so proud of myself. I was the hero, and I saved the day. I felt accomplished, not only as a good daughter but a big sister. I was responsible for all of us going to Disneyland. My dad even let me sit in the front seat instead of Cecilia.

Even though I knew we were right across the street from Disneyland, we drove around and around, all the while with Dad explaining how far away the park is from the parking area, and the first ride is the tram from the parking lot to the park.

We pulled up to what looked like a parking lot. As we got out of the car, Cecilia and I took off running, hanging onto my little brother. "Come back, come back, you're going the wrong way," my dad shouted.

There were so many cars, I couldn't see past them to see the castle. As we each struggled back toward him, he shouted at us again, but this time with angst. "Hurry, hurry, get in, come back… run!"

We were all running toward the car when he started shouting, "There's been a great flood, and it's headed this way."

Cecelia and I dove in as he began to frantically explain. "There was a flood, a horrible and dangerous flash flood. Mickey, Minnie, and all the Princesses drowned. Even poor Donald Duck is gone. The castle had been washed away, and there's no more Disneyland. It's a disaster."

We were all screaming in fear, and we begged him to leave so that we, too, wouldn't be washed away.

Now we all were in major tears and hysterics. Cecilia cried herself to sleep on the ride home. When we got to her house, she got out of the car, slammed the door, stomping and crying her way into her house. She didn't even say goodbye.

When I thought we were on our way home, we ended up at a park where I had never been. I didn't really notice what my dad was doing until he staggered over to the grass and passed out near the sand box where my little brother and I were playing. He stayed passed out in the grass until very late in the evening. A police officer woke him up; telling him it was too late to have us out.

When we got home, I thought my stepmother would be furious. Not a word was mentioned, not even that her baby sister was so disappointed.

This story became one of my dad's favorites to tell when entertaining company. In his many revivals of it, he would laugh the whole while and explain that when we thought we were in the Disneyland parking lot; he had taken us to a car dealership, one of the biggest in the state. He would gloat and praise me for being his 'little hustler,' making over $200.00 in only 3 hours, and as he would say, he "scored some of the best shit in that park." My stepmom got her share of the drugs, and that's what shut her up.

This was in 1984—there were no child protective laws against children pan-handling. To this day, Cecilia still hasn't been to Disneyland, and she still breaks out in tears and stomps out of the room whenever my dad tells this tale.

Everything to Lose
by Britney Campbell

I tried crack with my friends when I was fifteen. It wasn't like something you could just try. When you smoke it, you are addicted, and you always want more. The drug makes you feel so good that you keep smoking it, hoping to feel the same high you had the first time. My friends and I made a pact never to smoke it again. It was hard, but we helped each other to stay away from the drug.

I didn't do it again for years. Then the guy I was going with was doing crack and he always asked me to do it, but I would always say no. One day I just decided to do it. It's not like anyone ever made me do it. I'm not the kind of person who does anything unless I decide to.

The people who did crack would mess with my head until I would get all freaked out and didn't trust anybody. They would act like they were cops and then act like I was crazy because they never were cops. They played mind games.

And Then I Was Tempted

By this time, I had two children. When I first started smoking crack, I'd do it for a day or two, and then I would walk away. It was tough, but I would turn the ringer off on my phone so no one could call me. Then I was tempted, and eventually I gave in and smoked it. I was really screwed up and I would leave my kids with someone and didn't come home for days. My family couldn't deal with my long absences and ended up kicking me out. Once, I smoked it every day for three months, and would stay anywhere I could. That's when I got in trouble.

One Wild Night

One night I was at a fraternity party. We were smoking crack when I noticed they were putting something different into the pipe. This guy was going crazy and pulling knives on me and jumping in my face. I grabbed a dart to defend myself, and I took the pipe and ran across the street to flag down cars. A cop was coming around the corner. I guess somebody must have called him, but I didn't get that then. I flagged him down and walked up to the car to ask him if I could use his phone, or if he could give me a ride. He didn't ask me what was going on; he asked me if I was a street walker. I became defensive and asked him why, and he said, "Because you're flagging down cars and you have money hanging out of your pocket."

I did have money hanging from my pocket, but I argued, "So that makes me a street walker?" I then said, "I want to see your badge."

He said, "This is my badge," meaning his uniform, his car, and his picture ID.

I said, "I want to see the metal badge."

We ended up getting in an argument because he wouldn't call anyone to help me, and he had insulted me by calling me a prostitute. I thought I had the right to turn away and try to find help somewhere else. When I started to walk away, I got thrown on the ground. That's when he handcuffed me and found the dart and the pipe in my hands.

He said I made physical contact and tried to stab him. I was charged with aggravated assault on a police officer and drug paraphernalia. But later, when I went to court, the assault charge was lowered to simple assault, but the paraphernalia charge had been bumped up to drug distribution. They had to throw out the drug charge because I didn't have drugs on me.

I fought these charges for two years because I was so upset that this could even happen. I felt that I didn't do anything wrong. I was flagging down cars because I was trying to get out of a house where somebody was jumping in my face with a butcher knife.

I spent six days in a maximum security jail, and had two years' probation.

I came to peace with it after writing a letter of apology to the arresting officer. I told him that I was sorry if I hurt him in any way, and if that hadn't happened, I wouldn't be where I am today. I probably wouldn't even be here for my kids.

Although I don't agree with the way some cops are, my probation officer is awesome.

I'm Done!

My crack addition didn't end there. Living among drug addicts and making friends with people I shouldn't trust only led to more problems. A friend had money sitting out on a table and I told her, "Don't leave it there, because you can't trust these people." She told me to hold it for her, and I said, "I can't, I have to go to bed because I have court in the morning." While I was asleep, the people in the house convinced her that I was trying to steal her money and she beat me up. When I'd had enough of this kind of life, I called my brother because he's the only person I could rely on. I was done! I wasn't going to do drugs again! With crack, it's not like heroin, where you have to gradually come down. When you're done, you quit, and you'll be sick for a couple days. But the addiction is more of a mental thing, unlike OxyContin and heroin, which create physical pain. After I quit, I was still paranoid for a year. I was always looking over my shoulder, thinking someone was after me, or the cops were coming.

6. Cocaine

What should you do when you know someone is stealing to support a drug habit?

The ethical thing to do is to tell your thief friend to repay what was stolen, or you will be forced to alert the victim. This is not tattling, this is reporting a crime. Don't be loyal to a thief. Be loyal to doing the right thing—even if it means that you will lose a friendship. Integrity is more important than being accepted by a friend.

Brooks Gibbs
Teen Motivational Speaker

Facts about Cocaine

Cocaine is usually referred to as the powdered form of cocaine, which is usually mixed with talcum powder, cornstarch, powdered sugar, or drugs such as amphetamines.

This drug comes from coca leaves and was originally used as a pain killer. While it is usually sniffed through the nose, it can also be swallowed or rubbed on the gums. Some drug users will inject the drug, but this increases the likelihood of an overdose.

This deadly white powder is one of the most dangerous drugs known to man. Cocaine is second only to methamphetamine in psychological dependency. Once a person takes this drug, it's almost impossible to break free from the mental and physical effects. Cocaine stimulates nerve endings within the brain which create euphoria. The user quickly develops a tolerance, which can only be satisfied by taking higher or more frequent doses.

Cocaine is sold and used worldwide. Users include persons of all ages, occupations, and financial levels. Children as young as eight years old are addicted to this drug. Mothers who are addicted to cocaine give birth to addicted children. These children suffer from many birth defects.

Cocaine use can lead to breathing (respiratory) failure, stroke, bleeding in the brain (cerebral hemorrhage), or heart attack.

The most common street names for cocaine:

Aunt Nora	Mojo
Bernice	Nose candy
Binge	Paradise
Blow	Sneeze
C	Sniff
Charlie	Snow
Coke	Toot
Dust	White
Flake	

I utilized cash advances on my credit cards in order to help finance my habit. I couldn't get out of bed, go to class, or study without doing a few lines of cocaine. In time, I saw pieces of cartilage coming out of my nose.
Kevin Haushulz

Mixing cocaine with other drugs, such as tranquilizers, amphetamines, marijuana, or heroin, can cause a double drug addiction. This can also create a deadly combination which can be fatal.

Short-Term Effects
Short-term intense high
Followed by: Intense depression
Sleep/appetite problems
Edginess
Craving for more of the drug
Increased heart rate
Muscle spasms and convulsions
Paranoia

Long Term-Effects
User takes more and more to get high
Can become psychotic
Can have hallucinations
Loss of interest in activities
Willing to do anything to get the drug
Severe depression/suicide

Anger/hostility/anxiety—even when the user isn't high

*Information is used with permission from Foundation for a Drug-Free World

☼ **Start Anew** ☼

The Coke Man
by Rebecca Kanefsky

The Coke Man--Rebecca is also the author of "Disneyland", "OxyContin—AKA Hillbilly Heroin" and "Cheerleading"

My mother has an identical twin, Nana. When I was very young, I stayed with her most of the time. My mother worked full-time, an hour away from home, had an abusive husband, and they both were addicted to cocaine and alcohol. It was a hell of a lot more safe for me with my aunt. I didn't have my stepdad, Johnnie, there or his random biker buddies crashing on the couch in our one-bedroom apartment. I was always trying to figure out ways to stay at my aunt's house.

My aunt took me under her wing for most of my early childhood. Aunt Nana had two boys older than me, and my cousin Rachel was born when I was three and a half. I loved Nana like a mom, and Rachel and I bonded like sisters. My aunt ran a daycare out of her house, and across the street was the elementary school the four of us attended. Since my Aunt Nana was dealing coke as much as she was babysitting, my mom would show up to 'score' and either pick me up or drop me off. My aunt would ask if I could stay the night, and my mom would show up a few days to a week later.

I enjoyed staying in the house full of kids, babies, and my cousins, with the entire schoolyard to play in at any time.

Playing House

When Rachel was about six and I was nine, we would play house, like most little girls, feeling grown up, just like our parents. Now that we are both mothers, we have come to the realization that during this time, this was anything but a normal game of house.

It would start innocently, as most games of house do—the room is the house, the bed is the couch. We would set up her little kitchenette. The other bedroom was the baby's room with all their beds set up, and the closet was used as our office.

Before the game began, we would need certain things, like Smarties candies, baby dolls, a straw, a mirror, and something to crush the white candies with. We usually had candied cigarettes, but if we ate them all or just didn't have any, we would go into the ashtrays, take the cigarette butts, and use them. Since there was usually more than one brand, one would be a cigarette and another would be our pot.

Once we began playing, we would separate all the Smarties according to their color. The pink ones were birth control to prevent a pregnancy with a girl baby, and the blues prevented a pregnancy of a boy baby. The green ones made us sleepy, the yellow made us drunk, the purple were vitamins, and the white ones were crushed and snorted into a powder we called 'coke.'

The fun didn't end there. We would pretend the birth control didn't work and both of us would eventually become pregnant by the same 'coke man.' We would shove our dolls under our shirts and pretend to waddle about, all along arguing about whom he loved more.

When we played, we would snort and ingest our pretend drugs, all the while with our pretend babies in our bellies and even saying to each other things like, "You can't do this while you're pregnant. The cops will take your baby."

We coaxed my cousin Allen to play along with us. "You can be the cop! We'll even let you arrest us!" He would give in every time—he enjoyed it because we allowed him to rough us up and terrorize the bedroom before allowing him to take our baby dolls. He also liked taking off with all the candy . . . I mean, drugs. Any other time, we would tattle-tale in tears. As the story would play out, we would go so far as to have court, and he would then be the judge. We would argue and cry to get our babies back. He'd have us thrown in jail, all in a game of house.

Even though at this time, none of us had actually experienced being taken away or having our houses raided, our parents instilled the fear of the law in us and would tell us what could happen.

When we played, we would mimic everything we saw, such as sharing the cigarette we called our 'joint.' We would actually snort the candied powder; pretend we were drunk by slurring our words and stumbling about, and rush about cleaning the house and trying to hide our stash if there was a knock at the door.

Playing with our friends, we would ask them to babysit so we could go to the store, but when Rachel and I played, we asked each other to babysit so we could go to the bar.

I think it's amazing that Rachel has no addictions to this day and has never tried real cocaine or pills of any kind. Luckily, she never applied what she learned. She is so traumatized by what she experienced as a child, and so hurt by her parent's actions, she made a vow to her children and herself that she would never be under the influence while they are in her care. I think she is truly amazing. I have an addictive personality. Even though I'm not an alcoholic, I live as though one drink could put me over the edge.

It wasn't until Rachel and I were much older that we realized we only played this game together. One Halloween when she and I were nineteen and twenty-two years old, respectively, we got some rolls of Smarties at a party. We began to reminisce and told her mom all about how and what we played. She was shocked, and began crying and apologizing. We were so over it and had moved on, thinking we had learned from it. We tried explaining this is why we thought we knew so much about birth control, and realized we knew nothing.

☼ Know You Can ☼
I Overdosed Twice
by Erica Catton

Erica is also the author of "One Thing Led to Another" in the Heroin Section

I began smoking pot at age thirteen.

I tried cocaine a few times at the end of my senior year in high school. That summer, I was using just during the weekends at first, but then it became a daily habit.

Cocaine is an expensive habit, probably $80 to $100 a week. My parents owned a restaurant and I worked in the evenings as a waitress and used all my money to buy cocaine. I also had a second job, working all day holding a sign for road construction, and it paid really well.

I am from a middle-class Catholic family with five children. I became very withdrawn from my family and spent most of my time working and trying to support my drug habit.

I always snorted cocaine and never shot up. An addict is never alone in an addiction. There are plenty of others hanging around, and the drug was really easy to get. I knew a few people I could get it from, and we had one main dealer. We either got it in a small glass vial with the drug inside, or a small bag. It was about $20 for the smallest amount and up from there. A $20 dollar bag would only last a few hours.

Despite the fact that I overdosed twice on cocaine, I thought nothing would happen to me. The first time I was using cocaine and smoking a lot of marijuana, I felt the room start spinning. I went unconscious and woke up with blood all over my face from a nose-bleed. My kidneys hurt, and I was having trouble breathing. I was at a party and too afraid to go the hospital. Luckily, I made it through.

The second time, I did way too much cocaine and started getting really paranoid. I drove from a party to my parents' house at two a.m. and kept having to pull my car over because I was having anxiety attacks. I went into my parents' room and lay down at the foot of their bed, thinking I was going to die. That was probably the scariest time. I don't know how I survived, but somehow I did. I was definitely scared by what happened both times, but I was an addict. Even with these nearly fatal doses, I didn't stop using. I used less cocaine and would use other drugs more or instead.

I was never stupid, and was actually really smart, but just didn't try. When I started college, I almost flunked out of school the first semester, but managed to pass one class. The second semester, I did just enough to pass the classes, but still failed one or two. My dad then gave me an ultimatum. Basically he told me if I didn't pass my classes, I was done with school. My parents stopped giving me any money, so I didn't really have a choice. I had to stop doing the hard drugs.

Dad told me I had to stay in school that summer, pass the classes I had failed, and then pass everything from then out. I also had to get a job. At that point, I worked hard and got myself together. I started out with a major in Graphic Design, and then changed to Mass Communications.

I ended up with 3.8 GPA when I graduated, and thought my "drug days" were over. I still smoked marijuana on occasion, and drank.

Losing Control
by Jason

I think I am lost.
I'm taking these chances, not knowing the cost.
It alters reality, f***s with your brain.
And not till it's over do you feel the pain.

Once it takes over, you lose your control.
What you thought you could handle
Is no longer the same.

It f***s with your body, takes a piece of your soul.
The fun lasts awhile, but you still don't know.
If you make it a habit, you can lose your whole life,
The love for your family, your kids, and your wife.

Jason died at the age of twenty-four from a drug-related car accident, leaving behind a wife and two children. He is the father of Dillon.

I was first approached with drugs by a friend at age thirteen. I did take drugs but I stopped because it was ruining my body function. Now my plan is to just say "No." This is a good plan, especially if you are involved with sports.
Kenneth –age 16, from Philadelphia, PA

☼ **Find Your Strength** ☼
I Crossed the Line
by Kevin Hauschulz

Kevin is also the author of "Digging My Way Out" in the Rehab section

I can remember the first time I tried cocaine. I was on Spring Break in Negril, Jamaica, with about ten of my friends from the University of Connecticut. Some of these kids had previously experimented with cocaine. However, I had never tried it. At the time, I was experiencing anxiety attacks, and was feeling somewhat depressed. I sought to self-medicate and to get rid of those feelings in any way possible. While in Jamaica, I decided I would like to try cocaine just for the experience. As soon as I tried it, I fell in love with the drug. Normally, I am a reserved person, but cocaine enabled me to step out of my shell and become an extrovert. I loved the energy it gave me, and how quickly it affected me as opposed to alcohol, which took some time for its effects to be felt. I continued to use cocaine throughout the spring break in Jamaica.

Once I returned home to Connecticut, I wanted to continue to use cocaine because of the way it made me feel. In talking with some acquaintances, I found people who dealt the drug, at first in a distant town, and as time progressed, I found it in much closer locations.

The progression of my use of cocaine was very rapid.
• I went from never having used the drug before I went to Jamaica to an every-weekend user within a month.
• Within 2 months, I was using the drug almost every day. At that point, I needed the drug just to feel "normal," and some of the bad side effects from cocaine were beginning to take effect on me.

- First, I had gone from becoming a very laid-back person to someone who was constantly on edge, ready to fight anyone who got in my way.
- Second, my nose was constantly running, and was often times very red both from rubbing it and snorting the cocaine.
- I wasn't sleeping well because of the stimulant in my body, and so I was supplementing the cocaine with Xanax.
- I lost a considerable amount of weight and hardly ever ate, choosing to have cocaine be my diet rather than anything nutritious.
- As time progressed, I could not get out of bed, go to class, or study without doing a few lines of cocaine.
- I utilized cash advances on my credit cards in order to help finance my habit.
- In time, I saw pieces of cartilage coming out of my nose, and all the side effects I previously mentioned began to intensify.
- I sold marijuana and cocaine to support my habit, and friends that had been close would distance themselves from me.

In terms of my recovery, the seed was planted when I was in my senior year at UConn. I started seeing a counselor for some of the anxiety issues I was having, as well as the legal issues I had begun to encounter as a result of my drug addiction. The counselor let me know I had "crossed the line" to addiction and there was no way I could ever return to social use of cocaine. My denial was very deep. To prove I wasn't an addict, I forced myself to stop drinking and using for a weekend. I quickly returned to active drinking and using after showing everyone that I wasn't an addict.

☼ **GAIN COURAGE** ☼
A Party Gone Wrong
by Alicia, age 16

One Friday night, this guy I knew named Mike invited me, along with my friends Kim and Amy, to a party at his house. Most of the other kids he invited hadn't arrived yet. His roommate started raging because he couldn't find his 'coke'. He began pushing us around and grabbing our purses to see if we had taken it. We could tell by the way he was acting that he had already used all of it. He started shouting and came after us with knives he had grabbed from the kitchen. We barely got out of there—he grabbed one of my friends by the back of her shirt. With the help of our friend Mike, who was having the party, she managed to pull herself free.

It was cold outside and we were in a panic, shivering and crying because we were out of town and couldn't get hold of our parents. We ended up hitching a ride from a guy from a Middle Eastern country who didn't speak English very well. What choice did we have? We couldn't go back to that house—we were too cold and it was too far to walk. I told my friends it would be okay to take the ride, since there were three girls and the driver was the only guy. Each of us quickly found something we could use to defend ourselves. I grabbed my keys, Amy grabbed a small bottle of spray cologne, and Kim just planned to hit him with her purse. We told him to let us off around the corner from my friend's house because we didn't want him to know where we lived. He tried to follow, but my friend Amy threw her drink at his car and yelled, "Leave us alone."

He finally left and we ran to Amy's house.

7. Crystal Meth

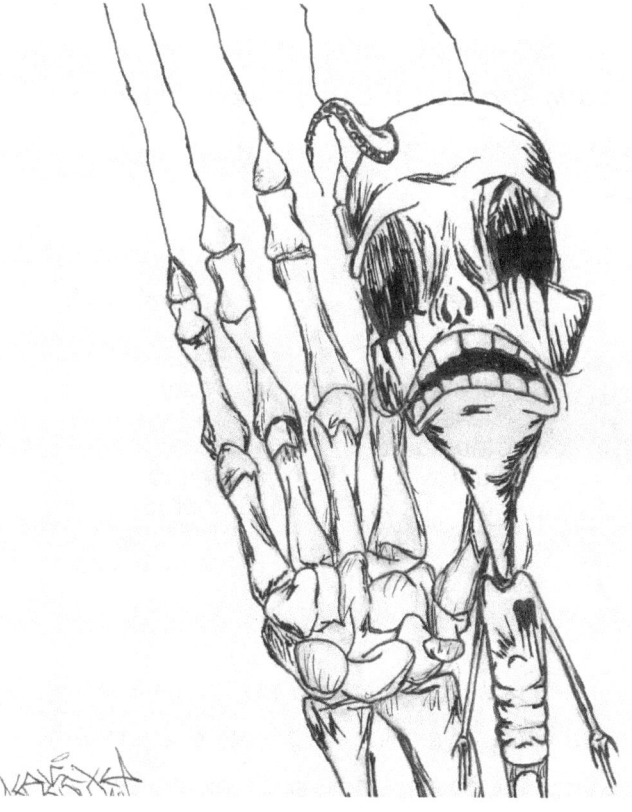

What do you do when you suspect drug abuse in a friend?

If they are really your friend, ask them straight out. "Are you doing any drugs?" If they lie to you—note to self—this is not a real friend. If they admit that they are using drugs, give them an ultimatum. "Quit drugs or lose the friendship." You can't be a silent bystander as they ruin their life. Offer to find them help through a rehab or addiction counselor. Tell them you will help through the process of recovery.

Brooks Gibbs
Teen Motivational Speaker

☼ **Start Anew** ☼

Facts about Methamphetamine

When we talk about methamphetamine, we're talking about a 92% addiction rate. If parents don't understand this, they're not going to take it very seriously.
Sherriff Tom Allman

Other names:

Meth	**Speed**	**Crystal Meth**
Beanies	Tick tick	Batu
Brown	Wash	Blade
Chalk	Yellow powder	Cristy
Crank	Glass	Chicken Feed
Hot Ice	Cinnamon	Ice
Crink	Quartz	Crypto
Shabu	Fast	Shards
Getgo	StoveTop	Methlies
Quick	Tina	Mexican Crack
Ventana	Redneck cocaine	

Crystal meth is short for crystal methamphetamine. Methamphetamine is a white crystalline drug that people take by snorting (inhaling through the nose), smoking, or injecting with a needle. Some even take it orally, but all develop a strong desire to continue using this substance because meth creates a false sense of happiness and well-being. The user also experiences a loss of appetite. These effects usually last from six to eight hours, but can last up to twenty-four hours. Although meth users talk about their pleasurable experiences with this drug, methamphetamine begins to destroy the user's life from the start.

Methamphetamine is an illegal drug, in the same class as cocaine and other powerful street drugs. It has many nicknames—meth, crank, and speed are the most common.

Crystal meth is used by people of all ages, but is most often used as a 'club drug.' It is taken at raves and night clubs. The common street name is ice or glass. It is a dangerous and potent chemical, and the poison that first acts as a stimulant begins to systematically destroy the body. This drug is associated with serious health problems, including memory loss, aggression, psychotic behavior, and possible heart and brain damage.

At first, the dealer offers it to you for free, but when you're addicted you actually go out of your way to find it. But then there are days when it seems like everybody on the planet is out of the drug. Those are the days when you're jonesing because you can't function without it.
Jennifer Parker

This highly addictive drug burns up the body's resources, creating a horrible dependence that can only be relieved by taking more.

Many users claim to be addicted the very first time they take it. The user can lose everything in the grips of this drug: home, family, friends, job, etc. Methamphetamine and crystal meth addiction is one of the hardest drug addictions to treat, and many die addicted.

This is a man-made chemical which contains such products as cold medicine, battery acid, drain cleaner, lantern fuel, and antifreeze—all highly poisonous and potentially explosive when being cooked.

*Information used with permission from Foundation for a Drug-Free World

☼ **Have Faith** ☼

Confessions of a Meth Addicted Mother
by Jennifer Parker

Everyone who loves me notices my drug problem, but I think I'm just fine but I forgot who the real me was, because these drugs have had me altered for so long. I totally revolve my life around them. I've replaced my loved ones with these fakes who call themselves my friends, because they accept me for who I am, and what I do. But this is not who I am, and the real me wouldn't do these harmful things to my body. The me in my head who tells me it's okay to do it one more time or it won't hurt me to do drugs is a fake too, and it's lying. The real me wouldn't lie to myself. The real me is the one who tells me I should not be doing this, I've got to change, and that God loves me.

I love myself for who I am, not what I do, or what I have. My family loves me for being me, myself and only me. *Written while Jennifer was addicted to meth

    I was nineteen the first time I took meth. I was still a teenager and I already had two babies. My husband was always gone and I later found out that he was addicted to cocaine.

    I was always sad and crying, looking out the window waiting for my husband to come home. My friend said meth would take my mind off my problems. I would forget and I wouldn't care anymore. Once I started using it, I lost the weight I had put on when I had my kids. When I didn't do meth, I put the weight back on. That made it even harder to quit, because I went from a size seven to a size three in about a week. When my husband, who was always telling me "you're fat," started saying, "Wow, you look great," I made the connection between the drug and looking good and it kind of stuck in my head. Everywhere I went, people would say, "You just had a baby? No way."

- **Did you know anything about this drug before you tried it?**

Not really. But when I tried it, it made me feel like I had superpowers because I got so much accomplished. My whole house was sparkling clean and I felt like I was Wonder Woman.

- **Do you think you were addicted right away?**

No, I wasn't addicted right away, because the first time I tried it, I hated it. That was about a year before, when my sister gave it to me, and we both hated it. I didn't like it because I couldn't sleep and I couldn't eat. I wanted to be able to sleep, but I couldn't close my eyes. But the time I tried it with Sabrina and I wasn't trying to sleep, I was like, "Wow."

Meth comes in different forms. In the beginning, it didn't seem so bad because it wasn't the crystal meth form. It was called crank, and it was more of a white chalky powder. Today you don't hear much about crank. Then I kind of got pushed into doing meth. It's pretty much the same drug in different form.

- **Is meth easy to get?**

At first, the dealer offers it to you for free, but when you're addicted you actually go out of your way to find it. If you associate with 'those kinds of people,' you're going to find it. But then there are days when it seems like everybody on the planet is out of the drug. Those are the days when you're jonesing because you can't function without it.

I always found a way to get the drug. If I didn't have the money, I would trick my husband into giving me money, or I'd take something he bought me back to the store.

I knew what I was doing was bad and I was ashamed of myself. Even though my husband always bragged about having a lot of money from selling pot, he wouldn't give me money, even for food. When he was asleep, I took money out of his wallet. I also sold some of the pot my husband had, but I never stole from anyone else.

My husband died in a car accident while making an out-of-state drug deal when he was twenty-four. *See my story in the Marijuana section: When I Grow Up* I was left to raise two children alone. During this time, I took over my husband's business, selling pot so I could pay my bills and feed my children. My roommates would take care of the children and try to keep me supplied with drugs. They didn't want me to be sad, so whenever I would think about losing my husband and begin to cry, they would put drugs in front of me.

It might seem good to have someone taking care of the kids, but they also stole from me when I slept. At first I wondered, *why would Kristen steal from me when I gave her a place to stay?* But then, she even stole from her own parents, so why wouldn't she steal from me?

• **How often did you do this drug?**

I took meth every day, unless I couldn't find it anywhere. If I didn't have it, I was looking all day for it until someone finally told me, "Sorry, we're not going to find any for a couple of days." Then I'd have to suffer. I would usually go to sleep.

I usually stayed up for 48 hours before sleeping. The first day is the best high, then you are dragging and your brain is fuzzy on the second day. I knew people who would do meth for days and days without sleeping and they would hallucinate.

• **How many days would you go without eating?**

I probably went two days at a time without eating, but I would always have to force-feed myself because I never lost touch with what I needed to do to care for my children. When you're on drugs, you can't stop eating when you come down. You do drugs, come down, eat and sleep, do more drugs, eat and sleep. That's all you do. While I was on the drug, I couldn't always get food to go down, so I would eat a lot of candy.

• **What is it called when you go off the meth and sleep?**

You crash! I wanted to sleep at least twenty-four hours, but with children, I was lucky to get sixteen hours of sleep.

I hid my car keys under my pillow, but my roommates would sneak them and drive my car around. One day, a roommate got into a wreck and totaled the car. Then none of us had transportation.

• **How long did your addiction continue?**

I was addicted to meth for five years. Five years might not seem like very long, but just think—I did meth every day for five years, from the age of nineteen until I was twenty-four, from when my daughter was born until she was five years old.

Each day I'd say, "I'm not going to do any meth today," arguing with myself. But then I'd do it again. It takes away your brain. When you're on meth, you have no real emotions. Nothing is real—you can't even feel 100% love on meth. You feel like a zombie, a puppet.

I kicked out all my roommates and my druggy boyfriend after the car was wrecked. I wanted to quit doing meth. One inner voice told me to quit and another told me that I'd gain weight and wouldn't be able to do anything. I'd be a loser. During that time I only did meth every few days.

One night I ate pizza and had the pain of my life. I had to call the meth-using boyfriend I had already kicked out to take me to the hospital because I knew he'd still be awake.

He took me to the emergency room. They said I had indigestion and sent me home with some antacids. A few nights later, my mom took me to the University Hospital and told them, "We aren't leaving until someone tells us what's wrong." We spent the whole night in the room, and in the early morning we were told that they suspected my gallbladder.

The ultrasound showed that I not only had gallstones, but a cyst on one of my ovaries, and a tubal pregnancy. I had to have surgery in a few weeks. While I was waiting for surgery, I tried to stay away from meth, and after the surgery, I had no desire for the drug. I felt like the doctor had "cut all the bad stuff out of me," and I didn't need meth any longer.

- **What saved your life?**

Prayer, the love I had for my kids, and the family who loved me saved my life. Prayer broke through. I had a voice telling me that I couldn't pray because of the way I was living. I wasn't worthy to pray. But I had to pray because I knew I was addicted and I couldn't do it alone. My mother and friends were also praying and fasting for me.

One day while my mother was praying, she heard a voice saying, "Jennifer is being healed. The people who know her now won't even know she's the same person." It's really true. I have never had a craving for the drug again.

I wanted to move from that house so the drug dealers and my druggy friends couldn't find me. My mom asked me, "If the devil came knocking at your door, would you let him in?"

I said "No."

"Well, they're the devil."

☼ **Realize** ☼

Face2Face with Meth
Sherriff Tom Allman
Mendocino County, CA

Methamphetamine is a real problem in my small county. When you look at the statistics, it doesn't seem so bad. The statistics have found that 4% of our high school seniors have done meth in the last thirty days. That means 160 high school kids have done meth in the last thirty days. With the addiction rate at 92%, we have 140 kids who are addicted to meth in our county.

Meth is a very cheap high. I'm forty-eight years old—when I was in high school, the kids who were trying to get high used cocaine. Cocaine is a much more expensive drug. Methamphetamine is 100% synthetic and it's a cheaper drug that allows kids to get the high for ten or fifteen dollars as opposed to twenty or twenty-five dollars.

The vast majority of the finished product methamphetamine comes from Mexico. Up until five years ago, we consistently had between ten and twenty meth labs a year in our county. However, over the last few years the federal government has worked very hard to put pseudoephedrine, you know the cold medicines, behind the counter. That has helped us immensely, because in the past, if they bought pseudoephedrine in quantity, it would take out two major chemical processes that they would have to do before they could finalize the methamphetamine. But now, because pseudoephedrine isn't as readily available in America, it is still available in Mexico, so that's where the finished product is made. It's then transported by mules and brought in by illegal immigrants.

- **How hard is it to kick the habit?**

With a 92% addiction rate, I know from the twenty-five years I've been with Mendocino County Sheriff's office that the majority of people who use methamphetamine end their addiction when they die.

In California, if traces of meth have been found in a home, there is a mandatory, legal disclosure for real estate. That's because of the carcinogens. When people have a meth lab, the chemicals get in the drywall, in the curtains, and of course, the carpet. I'm not talking furniture—I'm just talking about the things that remain in the house. If the home is a rental and the people have homeowner's insurance, contractors come out and rip out carpet, drywall, and anything that can absorb chemicals. It's very expensive.

- **How likely is it that kids will drop out of school if they're drug addicted?**

If kids are drug addicted, it's very, very likely that they will drop out of school. I have two teenage boys and as far as I know, neither of them has tried methamphetamine. My wife and I as parents talk about drugs on a daily basis. We don't point out as we're driving down the street that he got arrested, or she got arrested, but we talk about the physiological effects and the financial effects that drugs have on a teenager. It's very obvious that if parents want to be parents, drug use in their houses is much lower in comparison to a home where parents want to be a best friend.

For example: the youngest child I have seen on meth was eleven, and the drug was given to him by his parents. When we go out, to serve a search warrant, and arrest the parents on a meth offense, we call in CPS—Child Protective Services. The children are sent to a temporary foster home until the judge examines the situation and determines whether the kids will be returned to their parents.

If a child is born under the influence of meth or any other drug, the Child Protective Services is notified immediately by the hospital.

• I heard about the Face2Face Program while listening to NPR Radio.

The Face2Face Program is an idea I came up with to show the progression of methamphetamine. I called a software designer to design it. It's called Face2Face for a couple of reasons.

1) It allows us to have a face-to-face conversation with our kids, and we believe parents should also have a face-to-face conversation with their kids to talk about drugs. Not to talk about sports, not to talk about the weather, but to talk about drugs and sex. Parents have that responsibility.

2) It's also called Face2Face because we take a picture of a young person, which morphs into a picture of what they could look like if they were addicted to methamphetamine.

One of the reasons that it was so critical to use their own picture instead of a picture of someone else is that as a father of teenagers, I've come to the conclusion that many kids believe they have Teflon coating—problems are going to happen to other kids, but they aren't going to happen to them. It's not unusual to hear a teenage boy say, "Come on, Dad, my girlfriend is not going to get pregnant." Or "Come on, Dad, we're not going to get in a car accident. We wear our seat belts." The truth is, we as parents have the responsibility to help kids understand that they don't have Teflon coating. We needed to make this very personal to the teens, to show that they can be affected.

• Is there any way that other people can get a hold of your program?

In the world of software and cameras, it's fairly inexpensive at $3000. We're selling Face2Face to schools, police departments, and sheriff's offices all over the nation. People have heard the NPR program. They decided to give it a try and they've been absolutely astonished by the comments they're hearing from these kids.

We target between the ages of fourteen and nineteen. We don't really target the ones before fourteen because their faces aren't mature, so we'd have to do an age progression as well as the progression of meth. We will use this program for younger kids if the need comes up, but we don't want this to turn into a freak show. We want kids to be at a mature age so they will understand the seriousness of the effects of meth.

The most fascinating part is the reaction of the kids. We didn't know how this program would be received, and we have had kids ask us to come to their schools. Not principals, not teachers, but kids want us to come to their schools to show the other kids the effects they have just seen, with this program. It's really fascinating!

In conclusion, my soap box is for parents to be the parents and not the best friends. When parents were in high school and they were dealing with marijuana and alcohol, we're talking about a 9-12% addiction rate. When we talk about methamphetamine, we're talking about a 92% addiction rate. If parents don't understand this, they're not going to take it very seriously. And what we're trying to do is let parents understand the seriousness of this.

☼ **Strength** ☼

Worth Fighting For
by Crystal Atkinson

- **Crystal, you mentioned that you had a meth problem when you were in your twenties. How did you get involved with meth?**

I was married and had one child when I took a job as the assistant manager at Burger King. Everyone who worked there, including my manager, was into meth. They talked about it all the time and I knew they all did it. I had to be to work by 5:00 AM and I was always tired.

One day, Lisa, my manager, said, "Just try a little bit of this and you'll be good for the day."

I said, "No, I don't want to do that."

She tried to talk me into it for several days, since I was so tired at work, and finally I gave in and tried meth for the first time. When I tried it, I had a feeling of energy and felt wide awake and alert for the first time. I think I was hooked the first day. I wanted to do more and more, and it got so that I was using it five or six times a day. I would stay awake for four or five days at a time.

- **Did your husband know you had an addiction?**

Yes, he knew. He has never had an addiction, but he stood by me and never said he was going to leave me.

A couple times he told me, "This is getting bad. You need to get help."

The day I found out I was pregnant with our second child, he didn't even have to talk to me about quitting, I quit! But the thing is, I was still on meth before I knew I was pregnant. I was so upset to think I could have harmed my child. I thought, there's no way I can continue with this drug. I also knew we weren't done with our family.

• **But most people can't just walk away from meth like that. How did you do it?**

My kids have always meant more to me than anything. I can't tell you I didn't have some serious withdrawals. It was horrible. I would shake at night, and being pregnant at the same time and having the nausea anyway made it worse. For two weeks after I quit, it was just horrible, horrible withdrawals, but I fought to the end on that because there's no way I was going to hurt my baby and continue to do meth.

• **They would have taken your kids away if you delivered that baby on meth. Mothers don't just lose the baby—the state is likely to take away the other kids if a mom is on meth.**

If a mom keeps doing meth while pregnant, it's just selfish. I can't imagine being a mom, knowing you're pregnant, and going back to meth. I know the withdrawals are bad, but I could not do that to my baby. We now have three boys, and I have never touched an addictive substance again.

• **Good for you, Crystal!**

8. LSD

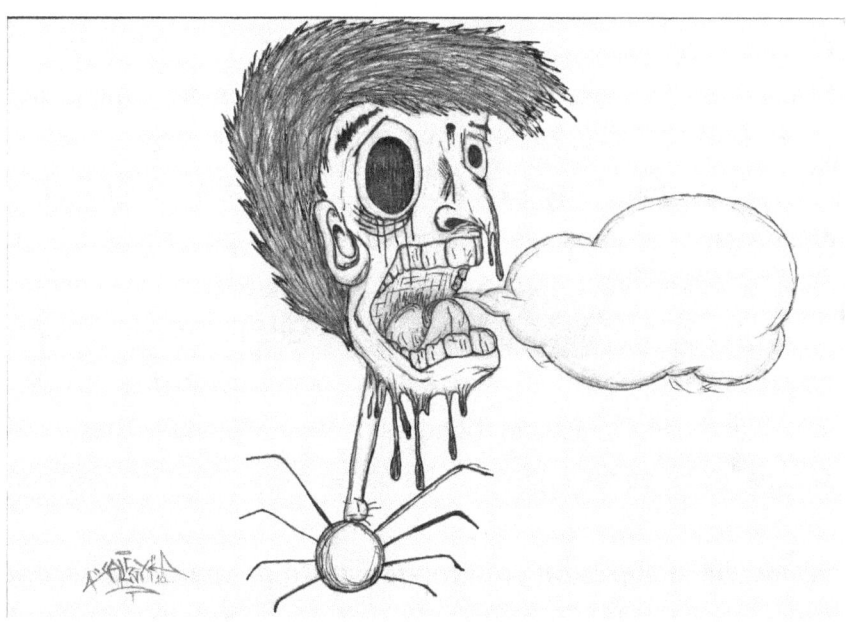

How can you find new friends when everyone you know does drugs?

You may have to be friendless for a time. Facebook may be your only social network for a while... and that is okay. By the way, if everyone you know is doing drugs, you are running in the wrong circles. Not everyone is doing drugs. You need to expand your social circle and visit places where good people gather. (Example: student leader clubs on campus, church youth groups, drama team, or try out for a sport.) Most people do not do drugs, so it shouldn't be hard to find a new circle of friends. It's not as hard or scary as you think!

Brooks Gibbs
Teen Motivational Speaker

Facts About LSD

LSD is a powerful mood-changing chemical found in the ergot fungus that grows on rye and other grains. This chemical, called lysergic acid, is produced in crystal form. Most of this product comes from the United States. Before distribution, the drug is converted to an odorless, colorless liquid with a bitter taste.

The drug, known as "acid," is sold in small tablets called microdots, or in capsules, gelatin squares, or paper stamps with cartoon characters.

No matter what form it's in, LSD leads to a dangerous disconnection from reality. This unreal experience of the mind is called a "trip" and usually lasts for 12 hours or more. When the user experiences terror, as they often do, it's called a "bad trip," or living hell.

"Once the stamp is on your tongue, the nightmare begins, and it's not something you can wake up from. You have no idea when it will end. I haven't taken the drug for quite awhile, but the flashbacks keep coming back."
Dillon

Street Names for LSD

Acid	Loony tunes	Window pane
Battery acid	Yellow sunshine	Boomers
Zen	Doses	Microdot
Dots	Pane	Golden Dragon
Superman	Hippie	Tab
Lucy in the sky with diamonds		

A Hallucinogen

A hallucinogen is a drug which causes hallucinations. The user experiences images, sounds, and feelings or sensations which only exist in their mind. Some hallucinogens cause the user to have sudden, unpredictable mood changes.

Risks of LSD

- The user can experience extreme changes in mood—anywhere from bliss to terror.
- The user is unable to discern whether sensations are coming from the drug or reality.
- LSD users distance themselves from normal life activities and often feel drawn to continue taking the drug.
- Some users experience bliss and may try to walk out a window several stories high to get a closer look at the ground. Others have walked into a busy intersection while admiring a beautiful sunset.
- While on a "bad trip," the user can experience fear of insanity or death.

When you go to sleep at night under normal circumstances, you can wake up from a bad dream. If you're watching a scary movie, you know it will be over in an hour or two—or you can walk out if needed. But there's no way to stop a bad acid trip. The nightmarish trip will last for 12 hours. Then it can start all over as a flashback, while you are driving down the road, trying to sleep or sitting in school.

Information used by permission from The Foundation for a Drug Free World

LSD scared me. It probably did the most damage of any drug that I did.
Erica Catton

☼ Be Aware ☼

A Handful of Candy
by Jerilyn Wheeler

One day when my grandpa took some laundry to my sister's bedroom, he spotted a candy dish on the dresser, filled with Reese's Pieces. He took a small handful of the candy and headed up the steps. He didn't know Stacey had put two hits of LSD on each piece. My grandpa had a nightmare with this drug that lasted for three days. He had been on LSD as a teenager and swore he would never take it again. He said this drug can come back with flashbacks when you least expect it. He suffered the ill effects of acid once again with his candy treat, and no one could help him come down from this hallucinogen.

LSD is a liquid drug. It is often put on stamps with cute pictures. Little children could lick a stamp to put it on a picture, and accidentally take drugs. Careless drug abusers put it on candy, and leave it lying around the house.

When you have people doing drugs around your house, don't accept anything to eat or drink from them. Especially watch out if they are giggling or laughing. They may lace your food with drugs in order to trick you into taking them.

☼ **ABLE TO CHANGE** ☼

LIVING RECKLESSLY
by Ashley Warner - age 22

When I was thirteen, my older sister and a large group of her hippie cohorts talked me into using acid. It was a small white square of stiff blotter paper.

Explaining an acid trip to a "non-doser" is like explaining child birth to a man. First, your world starts to get really distorted. You feel a type of chill throughout your body. Your vision becomes different. You see a "tracer" on things, like a multiple image following after it. For example, if you move your hand, you will see twenty hands following it. It is intense and becomes stronger. You "peak" after about 2-4 hours, but it lasts 8-12 hours, depending on the dose and strength.

The first time I took acid, I was so young, and I decided to go home, which was a bad move. I should have stayed around other people. I had to walk about two miles. On the walk (it was dark) I started seeing shadows. I got nervous, so I started making up poetry to keep my mind off things. I was cold and scared. It was late, and by the time I got home, I was reciting Jim Morrison lyrics. My mom knew I was loaded.

Even though I was so scared of acid, my band of idiot friends convinced me that I should give it a second try and they would look after me. Then I started doing it on a regular basis, without regard for my own safety. I even went to school f***ed up.

I once tripped for three days because we knew the cops were coming and had to eat all our drugs. See, it doesn't kick in for about forty-five minutes to an hour, so we knew we were lucky.

Besides acid, I was also smoking pot, taking mushrooms, and drinking alcohol. I don't really think I would have ever started harder drugs. I was living hard and doing extreme things. I was completely reckless with my general behavior overall, and the drugs were a large part of it.

I know I would have died from drugs and hard living if it weren't for my daughter. I got pregnant at the age of fifteen and gave birth to a beautiful baby girl when I was sixteen. When I found out I was pregnant, I just put it all down. I completely walked away from drugs and never looked back. I know my daughter saved my life. Now I have a good job as a med tech and I'm training to work in the ER at a hospital. I would never do anything to mess up my career, or that would interfere with being a good mother.

☼ Know the Dangers ☼
I Have No Idea How I Got There
by Shaun Albertson

I started doing acid when I was thirteen.

The summer when I was seventeen, I was going on a road trip with two of my friends to California. While we drove down I-15 in Utah, my buddy and I decided to take some acid. The driver was sober. My friend took five hits, while I took fourteen hits of acid at once. This was a lot more acid than I had ever done before. It took awhile for the drug to start kicking in. Although I felt the body high in about twenty minutes, I didn't get the visual effects until about an hour later. It was kind of creepy, because we were driving through the desert. It was really hot because the air conditioner in the car didn't work and I was sweating like a pig. With the weird body high along with sweating, I felt like I was melting. All the cactuses and shrubs seemed like they were walking. In my hallucination, I thought one of the cacti walked into the road. I grabbed the steering wheel, making my friend swerve around it, because I thought it was going to eat us. The other guy was tripping too, but I was just out of my mind.

Around sunset, the clouds began to change colors. They went from orange to pinkish, then purple, then green, then blue. All at once, the clouds came alive and flew through the air, like dragons or pterodactyls. I was kind of scared, but I knew it was just what the acid was doing to me, so I was able to keep it together. What really began to scare me was when it started turning dark. It seemed like the road we were on lifted off the ground. Rather than driving straight, we were going up, up, up off the ground.

During this 'trip,' I was smoking a ton of cigarettes, but sometimes I'd sit there with the same cigarette for about an hour. It wasn't lit, but to me it looked like it was smoking, and I kept taking a drag off it.

When I started coming down a little bit, I began drinking beer, and it made me so tired I fell asleep. When I woke up, we were in California, almost to our destination. It was really weird, because everything was really colorful. We were in a canyon and the cliffs and rocks appeared to be made out of chocolate. I kept telling the driver to pull over so I could take a bite out of the chocolate canyon. He laughed at me and wouldn't stop because he just knew I was trippin'.

When we eventually arrived at our friend's house in downtown LA, I took two more hits of acid. We were watching TV. It was really weird, because whatever was on the TV seemed like it was going on around me. For example, if we watched a war show, I thought I was in the war. I thought people were shooting at me, and I was really scared.

Our friend had a bunch of guys over, and we drank beer and smoked a lot of pot. While we partied, we were talking about going to Las Vegas.

The next thing I knew, we were in Las Vegas. I found myself walking down the Las Vegas Strip, with no idea how I got there. The lights on the Strip seemed to be bending down toward me in a sinister way. I almost got run over by a car because I ran out into the middle of the street, trying to get away from the lights which were after me. My friends pulled me back onto the sidewalk.

We all went into the casino, but they kicked us out because we were under age. The four of us found somebody who was really cool and he started walking around with us.

I drank more, and fell asleep in a hotel room. But when I woke up, I wasn't in the hotel room—I was in somebody's house who I didn't even know. None of the friends I had been with the entire time were there. I woke up in a real nice bed with a girl next to me. She woke up and tried to talk to me, but all I could see was her mouth moving. It freaked me out because I couldn't even understand what she was saying.

When I finally understood, she was talking about a four-inch cut on my back which was really deep. I had no idea who she was, how I got there, where my friends were, or how I got injured. Apparently, I befriended her in Las Vegas and went back with her to her home in St. George, Utah. I had already been there for three days before waking up in her bed. After hearing her story, I was pretty much sober. I was feeling hazy and had a very weird "Twilight Zone" feeling. I called my friend from my cell phone and he came to pick me up.

I haven't done acid now for years.

I'm glad I didn't fry my brain too badly. A lot of people I know had to be in a mental institution for quite awhile because of the effects of acid, and they didn't take nearly as much as I did.

Now I am a professional fighter in martial arts, but I haven't fought for about a year. I don't need a regular job, because every time I fight, I get about $50,000. I need to keep my body and mind in shape and I don't do drugs, except for occasional drinking. I hope to start working out again to get back in shape so I can fight every couple months.

9. Heroin

What should you do if an addicted parent or sibling becomes abusive?

You have to confront your abuser and tell them to stop. You can write it in a letter if you want. Be sure you make a copy just in case they don't listen to you. The most important thing you can do is document, document, document. You must keep a journal of some sort, reporting in detail about the abuse. This will be your evidence that this has happened. If they continue the abuse, you have to notify a trusted adult and ask them to intervene. If the problem still persists, notify the authorities. Don't let fear stop you from reporting it.

Brooks Gibbs
Teen Motivational Speaker

Facts about Heroin

I found my way to some of the worst, degraded places in the world to get heroin. I'm sure I could have died at any time from what was happening in this dangerous environment or from my addiction, but the same drugs that could have killed me fueled my push to survive.
Erica Catton

Origins of heroin

Heroin is an opiate found in poppies. Morphine is also a less refined form of opiate, which comes from poppies. Most of the street heroin available today comes from Afghanistan. Heroin was originally manufactured in 1898 by Bayer pharmaceutical company in Germany as a tuberculosis treatment which was also used to counteract the addiction to morphine.

First the addiction to opium became a huge problem, so the remedy was found in morphine. Next even more people became addicted to morphine so the pharmaceutical companies came up with a "non-addictive" drug called heroin. This solution became an even larger problem than morphine. In 1937, a German scientist developed what is now known as methadone. Also highly addictive, methadone is still used today as a treatment for heroin addiction. Depending on the age of the addict and how long they have been using heroin, many heroin addicts remain on methadone for the rest of their lives.

Is heroin addictive?

Although this highly addictive illegal drug is most commonly injected with a needle, some people are fooled to think it's not as dangerous to smoke or inhale heroin. This is not a drug you can experiment with. You may think you can try it once, but it will get you the first time around, causing you to give up everything of value in your life. You will lose family connections, your job, and your home and incur thousands of dollars in debt just to keep using this drug. Once it gets you into its grips, heroin will keep you, because the withdrawal is so extremely painful. Within hours after the drug effects decrease, the user will crave more. Withdrawal symptoms include restlessness, aches and pains in the bones, diarrhea, vomiting and severe discomfort. The only way to stop heroin withdrawal is to take more of the drug. The intense high only lasts a few minutes. With continued use, the abuser needs to increase the amounts of drugs just to feel normal.

Why is heroin so dangerous?

Heroin is cut with different products used to dilute it, which include sugar, caffeine or even strychnine and other poisons. The color can range from the purest form being white, to rosy gray, brown or even black. It is so hard to regulate the amount of heroin being taken because the user has no idea how much of the drug is included in the packet and how much is actually filler.

I quickly discovered that I could get a bag of heroin for $10, a fraction of my daily cocaine habit. I instantly fell in love with the effects of heroin, and was shooting the drug within a week. I had a series of three overdoses, all nearly fatal.
Kevin Haushulz

Street Names for Heroin
Big H	H	Junk
Skag	Horse	Smack
Thunder	Hell Dust	Nose Drops

Short Term Effects:
'Rush'	Slowed breathing
Foggy thinking	Vomiting
Sleepiness	Cold chills--from lowered body temperature

Coma or death from overdose

Long Term Effects:
Bad teeth
Inflamed gums
Constipation
Cold sweats
Itching
Weak immune system—getting sick easily
Respiratory illness—many require oxygen
Memory loss
Muscle weakness or being partly paralyzed
Inability to have children—both in men and women—even after the user has stopped using this drug
Insomnia
Aids, hepatitis C2, or other serious illnesses can occur from shared needles
Information used with permission from The Foundation for a Drug Free World

☼ Accept Help ☼

One Thing Led to Another
by Erica Catton

A tooth extraction and a prescription for pain pills started a downward spiral into drug abuse.

I had just finished school, and I had an exciting new job working for a magazine. I went home to have my wisdom teeth out. After the operation, I was prescribed Vicodin for the pain, and I was still popping pills after I went back to work. After a few days, I could see that I was starting to get addicted. I really couldn't stop, no matter what the situation was.

Within 4 months of my operation, I quit my job and moved back home. My parents owned a restaurant and I decided to manage it. They got me an apartment above the place.

After I moved back home, I connected with some "old friends" and could get just about anything I wanted. I was building up a tolerance for Vicodin and needed to buy more and more of the pain pills. A friend told me I could get a stronger pill for the same price I was paying for several Vicodin, so I tried OxyContin. It was expensive. I paid about a dollar a milligram, so a 20 mg pill (one of the lowest doses) was $20 and up from there.

When I built up a tolerance for OxyContin, I needed 80 mg to get high. That was $80. It seemed natural for me to move on to heroin, which was only $30-$40 and was stronger. I never shot up heroin—I always snorted it. Then, as I got more addicted, I started traveling to Philadelphia to get the drugs for $10-$20 a bag. I found my way to some of the worst, degraded places in the world to get heroin. I'm sure I could have died at any time from what was happening in this dangerous environment or from my addiction, but the same drugs that could have killed me fueled my push to survive.

I was managing my family's restaurant and working with my mom, my sister, and the best friend I'd known since the age of six. They knew something was up, but I don't think they realized how bad it was, at first.

I could handle my job for a few months, but once I was really hooked on heroin, I couldn't work, and I couldn't pay my bills. My life revolved around this drug. I couldn't even get out of bed in the morning until I did a line of heroin.

Can you give us some perspective on your heroin use?

Heroin is about $20-40 a bag. I would snort 4-6 bags a day. It's sold by the bag, but usually it's in paper, and the paper is folded a certain way to hold the drug so it doesn't spill.

How did you pay for the heroin? Did you ever steal to support

your habit?

I was in a position of trust, managing my parents' business, and I made okay money. I had no rent, as I lived above the restaurant. I also had an elderly grandma who paid me to help take care of her a few hours a week. I stole money from the business, my parents, and grandparents—really, anyone who would leave me around money. So yes, I would say I was forced by the habit to steal. It was like, if I didn't use heroin, I would get really sick. I couldn't get sick, so I had to use, so I had to get money. That was what I was doing in life. There was nothing else to me except my addiction.

Thank God, I was never a prostitute. I just couldn't bring myself to go down that road. I have met addicted people who have turned to prostitution to support their habit.

Going into treatment

Living around my family was really a cry for help. I was doing $100 in heroin per day when my family finally got me into treatment.

I went into the Narconon program, which is totally drug-free. You go through a drug-free withdrawal where they use vitamins for detox. I was worried that I would not be able to handle the withdrawal, since my body was so dependent on drugs. It took ten days to detox and I was really okay. From there, Naconon puts the patient through a sauna detoxification program that actually removes residue from the body tissue and reduces physical drug cravings. This has helped me more than any other process, because I no longer craved drugs.

The rest of the program teaches common sense applications and deals with life skill therapy to prepare patients to cope with life outside the rehab center. This is what really gave me stability. (More info www.narconon.org or www.stopaddiction.com).

I have been off drugs for eight years. I now work for a drug rehabilitation management company in marketing. I wanted to share my story to send a message to stop addiction.

☼ Truth ☼

Some Kind of Hero?
by Savanna Peterson

My dad spent most of my life in prison. During the short time he was out on parole, he would call my mom and say he was coming to pick me up. I was so excited. I packed my stuff and sat outside waiting for him for hours. My brother and my mom would tell me, "He's not going to show up", but I believed him and still thought he would come. My mom tried to call him all day and he wouldn't answer. He called the next day and said he was sorry, he fell asleep, but he would come that day. I would sit outside all day again and he still didn't come for me.

One day my dad just showed up. My mom felt sorry for me, so she let me go with him. It was morning and he said we were going swimming. I had on a swimming suit and he told me we were going into Smith's grocery store to get some candy and sunscreen.

Before we went into the store, he told me he was sick and needed medicine. My dad took out a needle and gave himself a shot, just like a nurse would. After he took the shot, he passed out in the pickup with the motor running. It was getting hot in the truck and I couldn't wake him up.

When a cop knocked on the door and asked if I was okay, I said yes, because my dad always said, "Cops are like monsters, taking your dad away for no reason." I was scared.

The cop asked if my dad was okay. He opened his eyes and said, "Yes, I'm just resting my eyes and waiting for my wife while she's in the store."

The cop opened the door because it was hot in the pickup. My dad and I got out and went into Smith's, and the cop left.

Later, my dad's girlfriend called my mom and told her not to let me go with my dad. She said my dad passed out and I was sitting in the truck for six hours!

It wasn't until I was seven that I finally realized what my dad was doing that day in the parking lot. One day I was messing around in the bathroom of our apartment, and I opened the toilet paper spring holder and found a [hypodermic] needle in the middle.

My mom was very mad when she saw the needle I found in the bathroom. She said it was used for doing drugs. It belonged to a man named Jerome who was staying with us until he could find a place to live. My mom screamed at him and told him to, "Get out now!" He denied it, saying over and over that the needle wasn't his.

When Jerome, the man who had been sleeping on our couch and helping my mom do dishes, left our house, things were missing like my mom's rent money, and even her deodorant.

My memory went back to the day I was in the parking lot with my dad when I was five years old. I saw my dad put a needle in himself. I'm not sure, but I think I saw him do it more than once. I think he did it in front of me, because I didn't know what he was doing. He wrapped something tight around his arm and tapped his muscle with his other hand twice and put the needle in. Now I remembered the medicine was called 'hero.' My dad would flex his muscles and say, "It makes me strong, just like a hero."

I was shaking all over when I found out that the needle in

the toilet roll holder was used for drugs. I turned as white as a ghost when I remembered my dad doing drugs in front of me. When I told my mom about the needle I saw my dad stick into his arm, Mom was very upset. She told me the drug my dad called 'hero' was really called heroin.

☼ **BE AWARE** ☼

A CRAZY RIDE
by Alicia - age 16

I wanted to go to a concert with my friend Kim at the Saltaire Concert Hall outside Salt Lake City, which is located in an isolated area along the Great Salt Lake. This guy we knew, who was in his twenties, bought us a concert ticket and offered to give us a ride out there.

I knew he smoked weed, but didn't know he had a serious drug problem. He had the radio blasting heavy metal music and began driving crazy, going over the line and nearly hitting a car head-on. We were scared and quickly buckled our seat belts and hung onto each other, crying, in the backseat. Then the guy would swerve the car to the other side of the road. He also sped up, then slowed way down.

While he was driving, he started shooting up heroin, right in front of us. During one of his swerves, the car bumped off the road, nearly flipping over, and landed in a ditch. He just sat there with a big grin on his face. My friend and I squeezed out through a small opening against the side of the ditch. The guy was acting so crazy, we kept looking back to make sure he wasn't following us. The music trailed behind us as we walked away from the car. We were on a highway, far away from town, without a ride. At this point, we didn't even care about the concert—we just wanted to go home. I called my mom on my cell phone and she left work early to come and pick up two very scared girls.

I was first approached with drugs when I was fourteen. I have since been offered drugs many times, but I have never done any drugs and I don't smoke. I enjoy shopping with my friends, talking about plenty of things and just chilling out at each other's houses.
Noelle—age 16 from Philadelphia, PA

My best friend was into drugs when I was thirteen. He wanted me to try it because he thought it was cool.

I said, "That's really bad for you."

He said, "It's a choice and who cares if it hurts you or not?"

I said, "Yeah, it's a choice that will ruin our friendship."

If people ask me to do drugs, I will say, "No thank you, I want to have a long and healthy life.
Brad—age 18, from SLC, UT

10. Inhalants

What should you do when someone you know has an adverse reaction to alcohol or drugs?

Take the alcohol or drugs away from your friend and call the nearest responsible adult to intervene. If they have stopped breathing or have passed out, call 911. You are not tattling—you are saving a life. Underage drinking or drug use at any age is wrong, but not helping someone who is having a reaction to alcohol is worse. If you help your friend who is reacting to alcohol or drugs, you are doing the right thing... and you shouldn't worry about getting in trouble for doing the right thing. Oftentimes, parents and other grownups care more about your safety than they care about punishing you for drinking or drug use. Doing the right thing is always a good idea.

Brooks Gibbs
Teen Motivational Speaker

FACTS ABOUT INHALANTS

The term "inhalants" refers to vapors from toxic substances which are inhaled to get a quick high. Use of inhalants can be called "sniffing", "huffing" or "bagging."

Some common products used as inhalants are shoe polish, glue, toluene—used as a solvent or fuel—gasoline, lighter fluid, and nitrous oxide, which is used in dental offices.

"Whippets" include whipped cream, spray paints, correction fluid, cleaning fluid, and amyl nitrite, which is used to open or widen blood vessels.

"Poppers" are locker room deodorizers, and "rush" is lacquer thinner or other paint solvents.

Street names for inhalants:

Air blast	Aroma of men	Moon gas	Whippets
Highball	Laughing gas	Thrust	Hardware
Snotballs	Bullet bolt	Poppers	Ames
Bolt	Oz	Whiteout	Hippie crack
Locker room	Toilet water	Heart-on	Spray
Buzz bomb	Quicksilver	Amys	Medusa
Pearls	Hiagra in a bottle	Texas shoe shine	
Huff	Toncho	Rush snappers	
Snappers	Bullet	Discorama	
Boppers	Poor man's pot	Satan's secret	
Shoot the breeze			

This guy I was dating took me to visit one of his friends. He took off somewhere in their house and left me in the living room. I found him in an upstairs bedroom with a bag over his

head, sniffing Pam cooking spray. I took the can and threw it out the window. When I got him out of there, rather than saying he loved me, he kept saying "I love Pam".
Jerilyn Wheeler

There are so many substances used as inhalants, and they go by many names. One danger of inhalants is the availability of these products in an average household. It may not be possible to hide all inhalants from an addict.

Some US states have made aerosol products unavailable to minors in stores.

* Information used with permission from Foundation for a Drug-Free World

WHIPPETS AND NITROUS OXIDE ABUSE

Nitrous oxide: a clean, colorless, oxidizing gas with a slightly sweet odor. It is used by the food industry as a propellant to make such items as whipped cream, and by auto racers to boost engine performance. Dental and medical professionals use it as an anesthetic; most people know it as "laughing gas." 1

Nitrous oxide is classified as an inhalant. One of the most common ways that teens abuse nitrous oxide is by inhaling the contents of small gas containers known as whippets. These containers, which resemble mini helium canisters, are marketed to allow individuals to whip cream at home. 2

A small but significant population of adolescents and young adults use nitrous oxide to get a quick high called a "buzz bomb," "shoot the breeze," "whippets," and "NOX." Regular users refer to the practice as "nanging" because of the repetitive sound distortions induced by the drug. Whatever its name, abuse of nitrous oxide is no laughing matter. 1

Whippets have been sold in convenient stores, and one California parent witnessed an ice cream truck selling them to junior high students. 2

Nitrous Mafia

Laughing gas in large tanks, like those used by dentists, has been smuggled into concerts, raves, festivals, and even sporting events by a group known as the "Nitrous Mafia." The group inflates balloons with the gas and sells them for $5 to $10. Those who buy the balloons inhale the contents to get high. When combined with other drugs and alcohol, the user experiences a high which will last for about three minutes.

Clean-up crews have found the remains of these balloons scattered among the debris left behind by those in attendance at such events. 3

Symptoms of Nitrous Oxide Abuse:

• Once inhaled, nitrous oxide reaches the brain quickly, affecting vital functions such as breathing and heart rate.

• It alters the nervous system and affects thought processes, behavior, and emotions.

• It can cause giddiness, loss of balance, slurred speech, twitching, mental confusion, and an inability to feel pain—which can be dangerous if the user is injured. 4

---

1 **Judy Battle**: Open Salon: **Nitrous Oxide Abuse: No Laughing Matter**
2 **Emily Battaglia**: Drug and Alcohol Addiction Recovery Magazine: **Signs of Inhalant Abuse**
3 **The Daily Swarm**: http://www.thedailyswarm.com/swarm/nitrous-mafia-real/
4 **Enotes.com**: http://www.enotes.com/drugs-substances-encyclopedia/nitrous-oxide/effects-body

☼ CHANGE TODAY ☼

No More, Not for Me
by Dillon - age 18

A friend talked me into doing an inhalant called Air Duster, which is used to blow dust out of your computer. Every day for about a week, my friend and I would inhale a couple of cans at a time. I only did it for about a week, and then I stopped because of a bad experience.

One day I went to the store to buy a drink with another friend. While in the store, I saw a can of Air Duster on a shelf, and took three really big huffs. On the fourth one, I held it in while I was walking away. I ditched the can on a shelf, and while I was walking, things turned funny. I began to hear helicopters just before I blacked out. That's all I remember. I felt like I was in a weird dream.

When my friend saw me take the first huff, he said a few cuss words and got out of there. When he came back to get me, I was passed out on the floor. He said he was trying to wake me up for awhile and thought I had died. I think I might have died. When I woke up, he was shaking me. He was freaking out. I got up on shaky legs and we were going to get in line to pay for the drink, but on second thought, we just set down the drink and tried to get out of the store.

A cop grabbed us and said, "Come with me." He took us into the office at the back of the store. He then called more cops. The cop asked me where I put the can. He said, "I was watching you on the monitor. I saw you pick up the can, but I didn't see you put it down."

It was then that he noticed that my pants were wet and assumed I had hidden the can down my pants. I admitted that I didn't have the can, and my pants were wet because I peed them when I passed out.

The cops looked up and down the aisles, trying to find the can of Air Duster. When they couldn't find it, they gave me a shoplifting charge. I hadn't actually stolen the can, but of course, huffing is illegal, and I did use a product that wasn't mine.

My mother was called to pick me up. I was given a list of charges, including shoplifting and intoxication. I guess it would be the same charge as opening a beer in the store and drinking it. They gave me a court date. And when I went to court, I was locked up in D.T. (detention).

I may not need to say this, but that was the last time I ever tried an inhalant. I could have died in the middle of Harmon's Grocery Store at the age of sixteen, and I wasn't dumb enough to try it again.

☼ **Remember Who You Are** ☼

Confessions of a Teenage Huffer
An interview with Crystal Atkinson

Crystal is the oldest of four children. She admits to leading a double life. In one life she was the sweet Christian girl who attended all church activities and summer camps. In her other life, she was messing around with deadly poison. The conflicting aspects of her life lead to extreme feelings of guilt.

• **Crystal, I understand you were addicted to inhalants as a teenager. At what age did you begin this habit?**

I was twelve and in junior high.

- **Did you feel pressure from your friends to try huffing?**

    Yes.

- **What kind of things did you inhale?**

    I tried several things, like varnish for cabinets, and even gasoline—but mostly Air Duster, which has a long straw attached and is used to blow the dust off computer keys.

- **How often did you indulge in this activity?**

    I did it three or four times a week.

- **Can you explain what it was like when you took this drug?**

    Inhaling Air Duster gave me a disconnected feeling, like I didn't care about anything. Nothing affected me. It was a high feeling, a not caring feeling.

- **How long would that feeling last?**

    It lasted about a half hour or so.

- **Did you drink or do other drugs along with it?**

    Eventually, I started drinking while doing inhalants, but I didn't drink until I was fifteen, but yeah, I did other things. I started smoking when I was thirteen, so I was huffing even before I started smoking.

- **Did you do a whole can or just a little bit?**

    Just a little bit at a time.

- **How did this activity affect your home life? Did your parents suspect there was a problem?**

    I started fighting with my parents around the age of twelve. I don't know if it's just the age—but it was probably the drugs. One time, my parents saw a news item about huffing and confronted me about it. Of course, I denied it. Another time, they found some Air Duster in my room, but I never told them what I was doing.

- **Did this activity affect your grades in school?**

    Yes, very much.

- **Did you go to school while you were high?**

    Yes, I often went to school when high.

- **I understand that you went to a funeral of a good friend while you were high.**

    I couldn't deal with the death of one of my church youth leaders, and I went to her funeral high. I felt guilty for a long time for doing that.

- **Did you ever pass out or have a scary reaction to huffing?**

    One time, I passed out from huffing and my mom called the ambulance. They didn't keep me at the hospital very long. I never told anyone what I had done, and they never figured it out.

- **Do you think one drug lead to another?**

    I did mess around with marijuana a little bit. I didn't start drinking until I was fifteen. I didn't use meth until I was twenty-one, so huffing didn't really lead me to other drugs, but because I had already tried one thing, it made me so I wasn't as hesitant to try other drugs.

- **How did you finally stop this addiction?**

    When I heard about a boy who died from huffing, it was pretty scary to me. I decided it wasn't worth my life. That's when I quit.

- **I know you have a lot of health problems. Did any of it come from your drug use?**

    You know, I've thought about it, but I have Lupus and most of it is genetic. I have an aunt who passed away from Lupus. I also have a cousin who has Lupus. I have been near death several times from organ failure, and now I have congestive heart failure and I'm only thirty-five years old. All my health problems are related to Lupus. If I didn't have relatives with health problems, I would think my health problems were related to the drugs. I started at age twelve, and that's a young age to mess with your brain.

11. Ecstasy

What should you do if someone you know is selling drugs to young children?

The best thing to do is notify that child's parents. Let them know that you want to stay anonymous, and then tell them everything you know about the problem.

Brooks Gibbs
Teen Motivational Speaker

Facts about Ecstasy

Ecstasy is classified by the U.S. Drug Enforcement Administration as a schedule 1 drug. This description, also used for LSD and heroin, is assigned to substances with no recognized medical use.

Ecstasy is illegal to manufacture, possess, or deliver. Penalties can include jail sentences from four years to life and fines from $250,000 to 4 million, which depends on the amount of the drug found in your possession.

What is Ecstasy?

The pure chemical form of Ecstasy was called MDMA and was manufactured in 1912 by Merck Pharmaceuticals. Over the years, it has been used by the Army in physiological warfare testing before being used as a psychotherapy drug, starting in the 1960's. In the 1970's, MDMA was first used illegally as a party drug. Today, the pure form of this drug is referred to as 'Molly.' Most of the Ecstasy on the streets has very little, if anything, to do with the original MDMA. It can include substances from LSD, cocaine, heroin, amphetamine, and methamphetamine, to rat poison, caffeine, and dog de-worming products. The cartoon logos on the pills make them more dangerous and attractive to younger children. A user may wish to take more of the drug to get higher or continue their high, but they can't be sure they are getting the same thing each time. They could be mixing a deadly combination.

Most Ecstasy is in pill form. The liquid form which is swallowed or injected is actually GHB, a nervous system depressant, and can be found in drain cleaners, floor strippers, and degreasers.

Street Names for Ecstasy

Cadillac	Elephants	Lover's speed
Adam	Eve	Roll
Beans	Hug	X
California Sunshine	Hug Drug	XE
Clarity	Scooby snacks	XTC
E	Love pill	Essense

I was insane. Here I was, an addiction doctor in the middle of a London ghetto, taking Ecstasy and going to raves. We didn't sleep for what felt like days. It was awful. I was hurting myself trying to get this man's attention and love.
Dr. Talia Witkowski

Ecstasy is considered a love drug because people want to touch and feel heightened sensations. Ecstasy is often mixed with a hallucinogen, which affects the mind in a way that the user will see and feel things that aren't real. The user can become stuck in a sad and scary place. Ecstasy is used as a club drug because of the extra energy and endurance it gives the user. This false sense of energy can lead to dehydration and over-extending your energy. Some young Ecstasy users have danced themselves to death, not realizing they were over-heated. They either pass out or die from heatstroke. You might think this won't happen to you. Do you really want to take that chance?

Short-Term Effects	**Long-Term Effects**
Impaired judgment	Long-lasting brain damage affecting memory
False sense of affection	
Confusion	Brain damage affecting sleep, learning, and emotion
Depression	
Sleep problems	Affects the nerves of the body
Severe anxiety	Acute depression and anxiety
Paranoia	Kidney failure
Drug cravings	Hemorrhaging

Muscle tension
Faintness and chills
Teeth clenching
Blurred vision
Nausea

Psychosis
Cardiovascular collapse
Liver failure
Convulsions
Death

*Information used with permission from Foundation for a Drug-Free World

☼ **Educate Yourself** ☼

Is This Your Candy?
by Savanna Peterson

I learned about Ecstasy at school during an assembly. Police officers came to talk to us about drugs. They took an old backpack from the lost and found and placed drugs inside. I think they were cocaine and Ecstasy. One of the cops hid the backpack somewhere in the school. The other cop took a dog around to sniff for drugs. The dog found and brought back the backpack. The officers then passed around pictures of drugs. The Ecstasy pills had pictures of Flintstones, Pokémon, Transformers, and even Barbie. They told us you have to watch out around your little brothers and sisters because they look like vitamins or candy.

I learned that Ecstasy pills can make you hallucinate. [The drug] makes you like to touch others and makes [your] pupils huge. I think it could kill a young child or a small animal, or at least hurt them. Druggies chop it up and sniff it, swallow it, or chew it. They even put it in their butt to make it kick in easier—faster.

Drugs were a big thing in the 60's and 70's. Now even nine, ten, or eleven-year-olds are getting into their parents' or older sister/brother's stash and taking it and becoming addicted or even dying.

One night while I was asleep, my brother had a party at our house. He often did this while my mom was at work. My little sister was only seven and I was around eleven. The next morning while I was making a bowl of cereal, my little sister picked up something off the counter. "Is this your candy?" she asked. "Can I have it?"

I turned to look at what she was holding. It was pink with a Care Bear on it. I shouted, "No! Kaitlin, put that down right now!" I grabbed the pill and ran to flush it down the toilet. When I told my little sister that it was drugs and we both realized she could have taken it and could have died, we both cried and were shaking so bad.

Kaitlin's dad called and screamed at my older brother, and then he screamed at my mom, but she didn't know what was going on. He called the cops, but they didn't do anything. I'm sure they patrolled our house and tried to pick up intoxicated teenagers.

☼ **Find a Way Out** ☼

Bombing on Ecstasy
by Dillon - age 18

My mom and dad went to California and I was supposed to stay with my grandma. I stayed with her one night, then didn't return to her house. She was planning to take me to Idaho the next day, but couldn't find me.

I was hanging out with a girl I knew, and we went to my cousin Brian's girlfriend's house to smoke some weed. Everyone at the house was on Ecstasy. I didn't really know what it was. Brian said, "Ecstasy is so cool—you should try it."

I felt excited to take it. The first time, Brian took a blue pill with a money sign on it and smashed it. He put it into a piece of toilet paper and had me swallow it. It's called parachuting. The next pill, he crushed and I was about to snort it when an adult came in with a drink in her hand. She freaked out, saying "No! You're not going to give that to him!" She should have taken it away, because as soon as she left the room, I snorted it anyway. Brian fed me Ecstasy all night long.

Ecstasy makes you want to move your jaw and your eyes roll back in your head. This other kid, David, was licking his lips so much that his lips were bleeding.

Somehow we ended up at Brian's house. The next morning, my grandma walked into the house, looking for me. My aunt was gone and everyone in the house was asleep. The girl I was with was asleep next to me in my cousin Savanna's bed. Savanna had spent the night at a friend's house. She would have freaked out if she knew we slept in her room, especially with her strong stand against drugs.

My grandma woke me up and said, "Come on, Dillon. We're going to Idaho."

Grandma told me later that I was staggering and got up with squinty eyes and said, with slurred speech, "Do you want to snuggle with me?" She said she was my grandma, and I said, "I know."

We couldn't find my shoes. Every time she tried to find my shoes, I would lie back down, and she had to start waking me up all over again. On our way, she had to buy me some flip-flops.

I slept in the car, then went into the house in Idaho and slept some more. I continued to sleep all weekend, except for when we went out to dinner. Grandma knew something was really wrong with me, but I wouldn't tell her what I had done. At first she thought I was drunk, but she knew that people don't stay drunk for three days.

☼ Fight for Your Future ☼

When the Wonder Fades
An interview with Mikey Rox

President of Paper Rox Scissors

Despite the control you think you have over your life, Ecstasy will render you powerless.

I started drinking and smoking cigarettes at age 15; I started using drugs at age 17. Interestingly enough, I hadn't even smoked pot before I tried Ecstasy for the first time. The first two consecutive nights of using Ecstasy led to experimentation with lots of other drugs, causing years of inner turmoil, torture, and torment.

When I was in college, I was using drugs (everything except heroin; my drug of choice was Ecstasy) and alcohol in excess, so much so that I was brought before the school conduct board, kicked off an extra-curricular activity, and was given an ultimatum by my fraternity brothers—attend AA and NA meetings, or face expulsion from the fraternity.

- **When you were 17 and took Ecstasy, what form was it in?**

It was in pill form. The first time I took an E pill was unplanned. I had wanted to try it for a while at that point, because I worked with a group of twenty-two and twenty-three-year-old people at the local mall who were very into the party scene and they told these stories about how great the drug felt and the glamorous nights they had while they were on it. So when the opportunity arose, I jumped on it. My first time was at a prominent local politician's house in Maryland. She was away and her son was hosting a party. A friend brought me there to hang out a bit, someone offered me the pill, and I took it. I knew it would be a long night—from what I heard, anyway, the high was supposed to last about six hours—so I told my friend to go home and pick me up in the morning. She did, and I'm very grateful for her friendship and loyalty.

• **You said you took your first pill. Did you only take one pill to last for six hours?**

Yes, the first time I only took one pill. I was wary of what more would do to me. I'm sort of a little guy–and back then I was even smaller–so one dose was enough. The intense high lasted for a good three hours, and then there's sort of a lesser high when you're coming down. It's the lesser high that gets you, because you want to be at the maximum high, so you keep popping pills. That's what got me in trouble down the road.

• **What did you like about it?**

I liked that the world in which I lived sort of stopped for a few hours. I was whisked away to another place. It was like nothing in my life mattered. My problems, my worries, anything that was bothering me was gone–it just vanished. And in that place was this feeling of ultimate euphoria. In the beginning, I thought, what's not to like about this?

• **Did these feelings change for you as time went on?**

Absolutely. In the beginning, E made me happy. It created a sense of peace for the few hours that I was high. I enjoyed that feeling. But it wasn't long before that euphoria turned to addiction. When addiction set in, the high wasn't benign anymore. In fact, it was the exact opposite. My smiley, happy disposition when I was high turned to anger and selfishness. At first, I enjoyed the company of others when I was rolling, but after a while, I became annoyed when I would take E with friends and they would talk too much or dance or sing or do anything that impeded my high. I wanted to sink into the drug, allow it to take complete hold, but it was hard to get to that place when so much was going on around me. I would get annoyed and very angry, and that attitude made me feel terrible when the drug wore off. I knew then that the drug was changing me.

- **Did you always drink alcohol while doing Ecstasy?**

No. The first couple of times, I was afraid to drink beer or liquor with the drug because I wasn't educated on the effects of the combinations. Despite that I was high out of my face, I still had enough sense to be somewhat careful—at least at first. I didn't start drinking on E until I had built up my tolerance to the point that one pill wasn't potent enough to get me as high as I wanted to be. Once I had gotten deep into the addiction, I paired E with all kinds of things—Ritalin, booze, cocaine, you name it. If it intensified or prolonged my high, I would take it. None of those drugs by themselves did anything for me, though. It was always the E that I wanted. I think that because I started out on such a heavy drug, the other drugs never compared. I used cocaine and prescription pills, but I was never addicted to them; they were always accessories to E—or drugs I would use when I couldn't find or afford E.

- **How accessible was that drug for you?**

Very. I had my own drug dealer, courtesy of my friends at the local mall. He would even give me a discount if I bought a certain number of pills. For instance, one night I convinced some of my high school friends to try it while I was home on break from college. I got enough of them to try it to buy 10 pills, and the drug dealer would give me two freebies for every ten pills I bought. His price was $20 a pill, but I charged my friends $25. With the free pills the dealer was giving me, combined with the extra fee I was charging my friends, I could have four pills all to myself. That scam really helped me get super high and build my tolerance. Do I feel bad now about doing that to my friends? Of course, but when drugs are on the brain, nothing else matters.

- **Was it expensive?**

It was very expensive. When the credit card companies started calling on my eighteenth birthday, I jumped at the chance to have every card I could. I put pin numbers on the cards so I could take cash out of the ATM to pay for the drugs. I maxed out two credit cards in two months by buying E. I didn't care about the problems it would create in the future—I just wanted my pills. It took me years to absolve myself from the credit card debt I had accumulated during that period. The monetary expense, however, didn't compare to the other things in my life that I was at risk of losing—my friends, my family, and my education. I very nearly flushed it all down the drain. And for what? Just to get high! That's the problem with drugs. You get so wrapped up in it all that you're blind or in denial that your world is crumbling around you. And when you do see signs of it happening, you just take more drugs to make it all go away for a while. It's a nasty vortex, and it will swallow you whole if you let it.

- **You say that you made it to college. Did you have trouble keeping up in high school?**

Not at all. I was always a good student. The drug problem didn't develop until I was just about finished with high school. Until E took over my life, I was on the honor roll every semester, had perfect attendance, was treasurer of the class for three years, served on the prom committee, was a peer counselor, etc. I was very involved, studious, and popular. I loved high school—and I'm so thankful that I made it through without the drug being a problem.

- **Why do you think your drug problem became worse in college?**

I didn't have anyone around 24/7 to keep tabs on me. When

I was at home, I didn't want my parents to find out I was using. They would have been devastated. But once I was at school, I could do whatever I wanted. Drugs were even more accessible, and I didn't have a scholarship that required me to keep up my grades. I could do whatever I pleased, and if my grades suffered, I could just blame it on the "transition." My first-semester freshman schedule didn't help matters, either. All of my classes were on Tuesdays and Thursdays. In my mind, that meant that I could party five nights a week. It was a terrible mistake—a mistake that eventually led me to the school conduct board.

- **Did anything change when you were brought before the school conduct board? Did you decide to turn things around?**

Things started to change around that time. That incident coincided with the extreme depth of my drug and alcohol addiction. I was brought before the board at the beginning of my sophomore year for convincing a freshman student to vandalize school property after a night of heavy drinking. I was part of an organization at my alma mater called the Maroon Corps, which consists of a select group of students who are recommended by faculty to become ambassadors of the school to help freshman move in and adjust to campus life. That's how good I was at hiding my addiction—throughout my freshman year, not many people knew I had a problem. At the conduct board meeting—in front of a panel of my peers and a dean—I was certainly embarrassed, but I was also deeply in denial. I was kicked off the Maroon Corps and put on probation by the college. But it didn't stop me right away. In fact, that was the same period of time when I had brought an 8-ball of cocaine back to school from home to share with my fraternity brothers. I was a raging drug addict and alcoholic at that point—and I needed help.

- **You spoke about inner turmoil, torture, and torment. Do you**

think there was an underlying problem that led you to drugs? Was the turmoil because you had let people down, or because you couldn't quit the drugs?

Part of my problem was because I'm gay, and at that period in my life, I didn't know how to handle those feelings. Growing up, I didn't know another gay person. I had never met anyone else who was gay—and everyone around me made it seem like homosexuality was a mortal sin. Many members of my family use the word "faggot" often and in its most derogatory sense. So I was afraid—very afraid of the feelings I was having inside. Part of my drug addiction stemmed from wanting to escape those feelings, and the realization that I am, in fact, gay. Equally, the other part of the addiction was because I wanted to try it. Those friends I worked with at the mall made it sound so amazing—and they seemed to be having the time of their lives, at least from what I could see. I wanted to be part of that.

- **Did your parents know you had a problem? Did they help you get sober?**

Not at first. I hid it very well. Like I said, I was very good at keeping up appearances. But when I got in trouble at college, my parents started to suspect that I was in real trouble. I think they suspected that it was all alcohol related. I don't think my parents suspected drugs—at least, not the caliber of drugs, anyway—for playing any part in my problems at school. At that time, it was hard for them to really know if I had a problem or not. I saw them maybe three times a year. And when I came home for break, I was out and about, visiting friends and getting high. I didn't want them to catch on, so I kept it far from them.

- **How did you finally get sober?**

Basically, my fraternity brothers put my social life and education on the line. After a particularly disastrous incident at a party—I had started a fight they had to finish—they convened to try to kick me out of the fraternity. Half of the brothers stood by me, half the brothers wanted me out. I knew before that incident that my life was spiraling out of control, but when I was faced with expulsion from the fraternity—which would have rendered me ostracized on such a small campus—I knew I had to shape up, or ship out. I thank some of them for standing by me and helping me through the recovery process, but I still sort of resent a few of them for indulging in all the excess—a few of them who wanted me out for my substance abuse had taken Ecstasy with me on several occasions, and others were snorting that 8-ball of cocaine in a car with me one night. I think it was a poor display of brotherhood, but overall, the entire situation helped me realize that I was headed down a deadly path.

- **Did your drug and alcohol use mess you up physically in any way?**

I can't be sure, but I do think the drugs have permanently affected me in some capacity. A few years ago, I had a CT scan and the doctor found a benign cyst on my brain. I think that it may have developed from my drug use. Otherwise, I don't feel as on point as I was before the drugs. Before the addiction, I was really poised to be something great—and now I fear that because of my indulgence, perhaps I've lost a certain edge, a measure of creativity that will always hold me back from being someone who does great things. I also feel like my body can't handle as much as it might have before. I truly think if I ever took another E pill, my heart would stop. Just stop. That prospect scares the s*** out of me, which, I suppose, is a good thing. I have a harder time concentrating and retaining information now, too. It's all very sad—because it could have been avoided.

- **What would you like to tell kids who are tempted by club drugs?**

Kids should know that when the wonder of it all fades, all that's left is disaster, despair, and sometimes death. The fantastic feeling you have for the limited time the drug is taking over your body doesn't compare to the years of torture it causes as you try to break free from its clutches to reclaim your life. After I beat my addiction, the most incredible feeling I had ever felt in the world—better than six pills high on Ecstasy, even—was waking up completely sober one morning. Ironic, isn't it?

When I was around eight or nine I lived across the street from a school. When I was in my bedroom I looked out the window and saw people selling drugs on the school playground. They were older, probably in high school or adults, but I didn't see their faces.

One day when I was walking with my friend Oscar, a car pulled up and a guy asked if we wanted to do drugs. We said no. Before we moved away from that neighborhood, I was offered drugs at least ten times, but I always said no.

Alfredo—age 11: sixth grader from SLC, UT

12. Prescription Drugs

How would you know if someone is addicted to drugs?

Addiction is, by definition, a persistent behavior pattern marked by physical and/or psychological dependency. You will notice the addiction causing them to fail in many areas of life.

• They will neglect their responsibilities at school, work, or home (e.g. flunking classes, skipping work, neglecting their children) because of their drug use.

• They will use drugs under dangerous conditions or taking risks while high, such as driving while on drugs, using dirty needles, or having unprotected sex.

- Their drug use will get them into legal trouble, such as arrests for disorderly conduct, driving under the influence, or stealing to support a drug habit.
- You will see major problems in their relationships, such as fights with a partner or family members, an unhappy boss, or the loss of old friends.

Brooks Gibbs
Teen Motivational Speaker

Facts about Prescription Pain Killers

What are prescription pain killers?

Prescription pain pills are usually included in the synthetic opiate category and react in the body in much the same way as heroin. These drugs are in the form of pills or capsules and are often smashed so the time-release feature is broken, delivering the drug's entire power at once. The abuser will either inhale through their nose, smoke, or inject these drugs.

Often, these pain pills are prescribed for pain following surgery, and the user continues to use them even after the cause of their pain has healed. Besides the dulling of pain, these opiates also produce a feeling of euphoria, or well-being, which is addictive to the user. If the user stops taking them abruptly, they will experience withdrawal symptoms such as restlessness, aches and pains in the bones, diarrhea, vomiting, and severe discomfort—the same symptoms caused by withdrawal from heroin. Prescription drug abusers often think that because these drugs are prescribed by a doctor, they are not as harmful as street drugs. This is a false notion. One of the main problems with prescription pain killers is that they are so easily obtained, and often over-prescribed. Children as young as twelve are addicted to pain pills, and they may be getting them from the medicine cabinet in their own bathroom.

Pain pills are so addictive, armed robberies of pharmacies have occurred. The robber isn't looking for money, but demanding OxyContin.

Street Names for Painkillers:

Generic Names	**Brand Name**	**Street Name**
Oxycodone	OxyContin, Percodan, Percocet, Roxiprin, Roxicet, Endodan, Enocet	Oxy 80's, Oxycotton, Oxycet, hillbilly heroin, percs, perks
Hydrocodone	Anexsia, Dicodid, Hycodan, Hycomine, Lorcet, Lortab, Norco, Tussionex, Vicodin	pain killers, vikes, hydros
Propoxyphene	Darvon	pinks, footballs, pink footballs, yellow footballs, 65's, Ns
Hydormorphone	Dilaudid	juice, dillies, drug street heroin
Merperidine	Demerol	demmies, pain killer

My parents really weren't picky about what drugs they would take. They mixed, they shot up, they did whatever their money could buy, whatever they could trade food stamps or other drugs for, or whatever they could convince the doctors they needed. And they did this as their job.
Rebecca Kanefsky

Ten Warning Signs of Pain Killer Dependency:

1. Increase in the dose of pain pills over time.
2. Change in personality—increase or decrease in energy, change in mood or lack of concentration.
3. Withdrawal from family and friends.
4. Continued use of pain pills after the medical condition is stabilized.
5. Doctor shopping—driving distances to visit multiple doctors to obtain prescriptions.
6. Decline in hygiene, change in sleeping and eating habits, cough, runny nose, and red eyes.
7. Not paying bills or doing household chores, and calling in sick to work or skipping school.
8. Overly stimulated by music, or having increased interest in normal objects and experiences hallucinations.
9. Defending themselves or becoming angry if their drug use is discovered or questioned.
10. Blackouts or forgetting whole segments of time or events.

Information used with permission from The Foundation for a Drug Free World

☼ COME BACK ☼

My Heart Almost Exploded
by Brianna - age 13

Last summer Brianna overdosed on Benadryl with two of her friends.

During the summer at the end of July or early August, I was hanging out with Lisa and Liz. Two friends of my brother's told us Benadryl would get us high. They said it wasn't illegal and it wouldn't hurt us. I remember one guy saying, "This is just like Ecstasy, but you have to take more."

We drove to Walmart where one of the boys and I walked in and stole a bottle of 100 Benadryl tablets. These are usually used for allergies or hives, and they work by speeding up your heart.

We drove to a wooded spot and stopped the car at the side of a road, while the three of us girls took 25 pills each. The guys then threw the bottle with the last 25 pills out the window of the car. The older boys said they weren't going to take any because they needed to make sure we were all right. I was so messed up because I'm the smallest. Trying to end up at my house, we gave directions to Lisa's house. Liz went to her own house and Lisa and I went to her house. They live next door to each other.

Lisa's mom came into her room. "What are you girls on? I know you are on something." We told her we weren't on anything.

I felt loopy—light and heavy at the same time. I had a hard time breathing because my throat was so dry. I had to keep drinking something.

She knew we had been with Liz, so she took us to Liz's house and called Liz's mom to come home from a meeting. Her mom came home and kept asking us what we were on. I was telling them I took Ecstasy, drank, and took weed because I was so messed up, I couldn't remember what I was on.

My friend's mother called my parents and had them pick me up. My mom took me home to change my clothes because I was dressed in short shorts and a top that didn't cover me very well. I told my mom, "Push F-5," and pointed at the wall, telling her to plug in the computer and push F-5. I also got down on the floor and searched for something I had lost, but I hadn't lost anything.

My mom drove me to the hospital. It was only my mom and me in the car, I don't know about the other girls. On the way there, I thought I was talking on the phone—but I was talking to myself on my hand.

When we got to the hospital, I had to tell them what I thought I took. I said I drank Everclear, smoked weed, and took Ecstasy. I had been on them before; I can't lie. The nurse took a urine sample and a blood test to make sure I hadn't taken an illegal substance. Then she gave me an IV, with something in it to slow down my heart rate and rehydrate me. Benadryl dries you up so much.

Someone came into the hospital room and told my mom I had antihistamine in my system. The nurse brought in a lady to talk to me and ask if I needed a counselor. She thought I was trying to kill myself. I said, "No, I was just trying to get high."

After that, the doctor told my mom that my heart rate was 150, and if she hadn't brought me to the hospital, I would have died. My heart would have exploded!

We took our pictures together that night before we overdosed. Later I found out that both of my friends also ended up in the hospital. That was the worst experience of my life and now we want to hang out with Savanna Peterson more, because she's drug free, and we want to stay away from drugs. I don't want to do drugs again.

☼ EDUCATE YOURSELF ☼

AN INTERVIEW WITH A PHARMACIST
Ryan Farmer
Pharmacy Manager, Sam's Club

- **What are the most abused prescription drugs?**

OxyContin, Lortab, Xanax, Valium, and Percocet are the most commonly abused prescription drugs.

- **Are people starting out by being prescribed these drugs, or are they taking someone else's prescription?**

I'd say both. Maybe they were prescribed them long-term and they eventually abused them, or they right away start to abuse them after hearing about it from someone else. They might go and rob people to get it, or take it from their parents.

- **How many times a day, on average, are these drugs being taken by an abuser?**

Depending on the medication—OxyContin is usually prescribed to be taken twice a day. But people who abuse them probably do it six or seven times a day. Lortab is taken probably five or six times a day [for pain]. An abuser probably will take it ten to fifteen times a day.

- **What does the prescription medication do to the abuser?**

They get the euphoria effect. It gives them that buzz, that high effect that they are looking for. For some people it just takes away their worries. They have a feeling of no worries, everything is good, they like being on it and don't like it when it wears off, so they start to abuse it.

- **Do they need more and more to get the same feeling?**

Yes, because people build up tolerance to these medications, so months down the road, one pill goes into three pills to get that same high. Then four, then five, and so on.

• **Why do you think this problem is so wide-spread?**

Because people who are on prescription meds don't think it is as bad as, say, marijuana, cocaine, and heroin. They think, "It's a prescription, so it's okay." I think they also want to feel that high.

• **Some who abuse prescription drugs are older, right?**

Older people might feel they have too much stress in their life, or it was prescribed for them. There are a lot of different reasons why people actually do it.

• **How hard is it to kick this habit?**

Very hard! I'd say anything you're addicted to, spending money or any habit is hard to get off. It's worse with drugs, because it actually causes a chemical reaction in your body. Some people like to just go cold turkey, while others have to slowly wean themselves off. It really depends on if the person wants to stop. If they know they have a problem and want to get off, they can get off in a month.

• **I heard that withdrawal from some drugs can be fatal. To which drugs does this apply?**

It can apply to any of these drugs if they are to stop cold turkey. There are rebound effects of the withdrawal. They can suffer anxiety and go through anger, irritation, and cold sweats, and their heart rate goes up. They can actually have seizures. That's why it's good for people to wean themselves off it slowly.

• **Are there medications that can be given to help with withdrawal?**

Yes, there are quite a few that can help. They can also, instead of taking ten Lortab a day, cut down to five a day for maybe two or three days, and slowly work themselves off. They can stay on the same medication, or they can switch to a totally different one that is actually designed to help treat people who are on these kinds of medications.

☼ Find Your True Self ☼

Overdoing It
An Interview with Dez - age 26

Dez began smoking cigarettes at age 12. He started drinking and smoking weed at 14. You will also find an interview with Dez in the Alcohol section titled: "It's Always Going to Haunt Me" in the Alcohol section.

I've been down and out so many times, but now I'm doing so much better because I made the decision to stop using. It's a rough road, especially for people who don't know how and don't have the mind power. Especially being young, kids don't understand the consequences of drug use. The main problem is opiates, such as heroin, Vicodin, Percocet, Darvoset; any of that type of medication. OxyContin is especially bad.

- **Were you addicted to OxyContin?**

I was having problems with that for awhile, which only got worse when I realized you could smoke the pills. It gives you such anxiety when you're coming off it. You can't sleep, you get nervous shakes, and you get hot and cold sweats. It's just horrible, and some people will smoke four or five of them a day.

- **How do they smoke it? Do they put it into a cigarette or something?**

They smoke it in foil. They just smoke it as-is. That's one of the new things going on right now. I've never shot up, so I don't know what that feels like. There are a lot of people who are really,

really stuck on shooting up OxyContin. They call it the "intravenous pathology."

- **How did somebody talk you into taking it in the first place?**

Nobody talked me into it. Somebody just had it, and I said, "I'll try." Peer pressure is not about the peers, it's about you wanting to fit in with the peers.

- **How did you get hold of the pills?**

You can find them anywhere. I'm a very personable person and I can spot people who are high. Once you've done it, you can just kind of tell, they're 'speeded.' It's easy once you've been in the game a little bit, just finding drugs.

- **When you would take OxyContin, how many pills would you take per day?**

People's body chemistries are so different. I'm a big guy, at 225 lbs. How much I'd take would depend on my tolerance. I might take one the first day and take two the next day, then increase the dose to three. Someone who has never taken it before can take a tiny little bit and get high. What I've found is that some people can take six, seven, or eight pills and drink along with it. They become criminal at that point because they can't afford their habit. I know a couple people who are involved in the trafficking. There's a lot of denial about hurting people. I've expressed to them, "You're the ones who are doing this to us."

- **But they're probably supporting their own habit by selling it.**

It's surprising but from my experience, most of those who sell it don't do it.

- **What do you know about doctor shoppers?**

Drug abusers are the ones who control the doctor. Once you're educated and know what you want, you can tell the doctor anything and they'll prescribe it for you. You can pretty much lie.

I've gotten prescribed things before just by acting like I was having a panic attack. A lot of people are actors. I don't necessarily bash prescription drugs—it's just that there are so many of them being prescribed.

A couple of big-time doctors, people would just go to for prescriptions, have been caught. People would pay them money and they would write out a prescription, and then the pharmaceutical companies make their money because they charge like $10 a pill, and the value is much higher when people sell them on the street. So the pharmaceutical companies up the price. As long as they can still pump the drugs out, it's fine for them. It's the same thing with Ritalin, Adderall, uppers, downers, muscle relaxers—the list can go on and on.

- **It's not just that they're being prescribed, but they're getting them off the street.**

They're not necessarily being prescribed to take them—they're getting prescriptions and selling them to make money. They have insurance. Insurance covers the majority of pills. People have surgeries and they are prescribed these strong pain pills. When they don't need them anymore, they keep saying that they do need them.

I've also seen that when someone is using, they'll have what you call "the nods." They'll be passed out and their neck will be bent over. They could be like that for an hour or two. They'll wake up and their neck is hurting like crazy. First they use, then they pass out. When they wake up, their back and neck are hurting, so they'll go back to the doctor for more pain pills. It's a never-ending cycle.

- **How expensive is the habit?**

An OxyContin addiction can cost over $1000 a week, once your tolerance goes up. The price goes up and up. I've heard that

Xanax is just as bad. When you can't find the drug, your body hurts—it hurts. People tend to become suicidal when coming down from these drugs. When people can't get them, they start freaking out.

• **So, have you taken all the pills you mentioned?**

Yeah, I've taken them all. It would just depend on whether I wanted to feel high or low or a little sideways. If I needed to clean the house, I'd take an upper. If I needed to relax, I'd take a downer.

• **Maybe you could just drink coffee…**

I used to, but it hurts my intestines. I drank too much of it. It also gets my heart racing.

• **So even coffee was an addiction, because you overdid it.**

Yeah, I'm always overdoing it. That's just my personality. Some days I lay around playing video games. It's an addiction because it affects you. I literally dream my video games. It's like when you fall asleep with a movie playing, and you start dreaming about the movie. Even though you're not concentrating on the movie, you still hear it while you sleep. It's like that with drugs, when you're unconscious your subconscious takes over.

• **What have you lost because of your addictions? Have you lost a job or school, respect of your family, an apartment, or relationships?**

Oh, yes, numerous times—I've lost all those things. Now I don't even get into a relationship because of my problems. I've been single for awhile now, just because I don't want to involve anyone in it. It's not worth it to me to just drag someone else down. If I can't take care of myself, how can I take care of anyone else?

• **A lot of people try to hide their drug problems from their families. Are your parents aware of your drug problems?**

I think people hide their addictions because they don't want to be ashamed. To me, shame is just how you make yourself feel. I'm not really ashamed of what I've done, because I've done it, and how am I going to change that? Why feel that shame? Only actions are going to change things.

I 'fessed up to my parents. If there's anyone you should be honest with, it's your parents. We're a strong family. But when people tell me not to do something, I do it more. That's my personality. My stepfather had problems with drugs years and years ago. He's been clean for over twenty years. When my family gets after me about my drinking, I go to meetings to help me cope with sobriety.

During the times when I've been sober, I could go into a bar and not drink by appointing myself as the designated driver. This was possible for me because I cared about the people I was with.

- **You're still putting yourself in an uncomfortable situation.**

Well, there are always going to be uncomfortable situations. You can't just put yourself away from that. You've got to be strong enough to be around it, and not do it. If it comes around, all you need to have is some money in your pocket and someone to buy it from. Right there is the temptation. You can find drugs anywhere. It's just my choice now that I don't want to look for them. That makes it a lot easier to stay clean, without trying to go searching. That's kind of made me into a homebody. It's stabilized me a little bit, especially having my mom pulling for me.

☼ **Maintain** ☼

OxyContin—aka Hillbilly Heroin
by Rebecca Kanefsky

Rebecca is the author of the following stories:, "Disneyland", "The Coke Man" and "Cheerleading"

I am the thirty-four-year-old daughter of a father who was addicted to heroin, methadone, and whatever kind of pills he can scrounge enough money together to get, and a mother who favored cocaine in the 80's, while alcohol has seen her through to today.

I had a very tumultuous childhood, living in L.A. with my mother and her abusive husband Johnnie until I was ten. They were heavy into cocaine and drinking. After one of our major beatings, I gave my mother the choice of me or him. She chose him. This was during the D.A.R.E. campaign. When the police officer asked the kids if anyone had seen drugs, I raised my hand and proceeded to divulge a lot of my families' personal information. Before the end of that school day, a SWAT team moved in and raided my house. I was in foster care for a week before my uncle on my father's side took me in for a little over 3 months, and one day my mom came and picked me up with a suitcase and took me to the airport.

At age ten, I moved to Kentucky and lived with my father and step-mother until I was 18. My mother was well aware my dad and stepmom were junkies/heroin addicts. She also knew that no one in the home was working and they were drug runners and doctor shoppers, and that welfare was the only breadwinner in the home. When I asked my mother why she allowed me to stay with my dad, under these circumstances, her reply was, "He's your dad. He wouldn't do anything to hurt you."

Drugs were very prevalent in our town, and it was obvious that my dad was selling. People in town not only saw him staggering around, high, but they also saw him going around town making drug deals. The drug of choice in Rural Appalachia, Kentucky was "Hillbilly Heroin," which is OxyContin. My dad and step-mom would even go so far as to injure themselves in order to get a doctor to give them pain pills.

My parents really weren't picky about what drugs they would take. They mixed, they shot up, they did whatever their money could buy, whatever they could trade food stamps or other drugs for, or whatever they could convince the doctors they needed.

13. Rehab

How can you make a difference for a person who is drug addicted?

In Savanna's Words: "I do believe in change and a second chance. People who do drugs need a second chance because if everyone gives up on them, they're going to give up on life and pretty much overdose. Then people will feel horrible because they gave up and didn't give them another chance. Everybody deserves it."

In Eryn's Words: "Not giving up doesn't mean you hang out with them when they're doing drugs, but you could offer them other activities—like 'let's go to a movie, or let's go hang out at my house tonight. If you want to come, we'll be there all night.'" Eryn Gorang is a member of Peer Leadership Team.

All my life I had avoided pain as best I could, but now I knew I had actually caused myself more pain by doing so. In that mo-

ment at the mall, I was ready for a solution, and I was willing to change.

Kristen Moeller, author: "Waiting for Jack"

While a patient cannot die from withdrawal of narcotics or stimulants, withdrawal can be highly dangerous and, in the case of alcohol and benzodiazepine abuse, if detoxification is not monitored carefully by a physician, the patient could die.

Dr. Punyamurtula Kishore, PMA President, President of the National Library of Addictions

☼ **BELIEVE IN YOURSELF** ☼

The Way an Addict Thinks
by Scott Gaba, C.A.T.C., C.D.S.

Not everyone does drugs. Some people think everyone is getting high—they aren't. Only about 15% of high school students are doing drugs.

I am a counselor, and I have been in recovery for thirty-two years. I work with outpatients who are in early recovery. I also work in the entertainment industry.

I'm an alcoholic. I hit bottom and had nine years clean. I picked up a drink and it was as if I had never quit. Now I'm sober and I want to help others. I'm in recovery; I have gone through 12-step programs.

Drug and alcohol abuse runs in a family and is passed on from generation to generation. My dad was an addict and my mother is an overeater in denial. This pattern goes down to my nieces, nephews, and more.

People with normal thinking don't put something in their bodies to feel different. Normal people may take a drink once in a while. If you are a blackout drinker, you cross that line. You will drink to that limit again, hurt yourself, or hurt someone else.

If you have an everyday habit, you must not like something about yourself and you're trying to cover it up. Once you find and fix the problem, you won't need to drink away your sorrows. You can go to a 12-step program or go to a church, temple or synagogue—just don't go back to the drug. With addiction, there is so much denial, loneliness, and 'low bottoms' where you can lose everything. The only place left to go is up, and up is sobriety. Drug addicts end up in jails, in institutions, or dead.

Alcohol is a chronic brain-relapsing disease. If a person put a hand on a burner and burned their hand, they wouldn't do it again. The addict's perception is different from that of others. Addicts would forget and do it again, thinking they would have a different result. The warped thinking is caused by the disease.

Addicts are highly creative people. I work in Hollywood as a costumer, dressing stars for TV and the movies. When I was drinking, I lost my position in Hollywood, because nothing was more important to me than alcohol. I changed my life and a studio took a chance on me. Without the drug, I now have a higher position than I had before. I am a costume supervisor for Warner Brothers.

My dad was also a costumer in Hollywood. He took his own life because of the disease of alcoholism.

Although a job in Hollywood seems glamorous, my passion is working with addicts. My brother and I ran a men and women's sober living house for four years, and I am very proud of our work there. Now I am following my dream. I have been in school for three years and will soon be licensed as a counselor.

☼ **Accept Help** ☼

Treating Addiction as a Disease
Dr. Punyamurtula Kishore

National Library of Addictions (NLA) President and President of Preventive Medicine Associates, Inc. (PMA). PMA is a group of family practices located throughout Massachusetts.

• **Dr. Kishore, I am very interested in the concept that addiction is a disease, rather than a social problem. Will you explain this theory?**

Addiction is a disease that can afflict any person regardless of age, race, gender, creed, or socioeconomic status. Addiction affects the whole body and mind, and thus, we must treat the whole patient. Our 40+ Preventative Medicine Associates offices across Massachusetts treat the physical with primary care and internal medicine techniques and tackle the social and mental aspects with individual and group counseling. We also offer a unique range of mental health services at our Neuroscience Center. We then work to educate the patients on how to keep healthy and avoid relapse.

It's important to note that addiction is a *lifelong* illness. There is no time frame or limit on the care we provide. Patients can come to us for quality treatment for as long as they like or need.

The effects of addiction on social systems has helped shape the generally held view that drug dependence is primarily a social problem, not a health problem. In turn, medical approaches to prevention and treatment are lacking.

Thomas McLellan, PhD, and others examined evidence that drug and alcohol addiction is a chronic medical illness. They published their finding in the October 4, 2000 issue of the *Journal of the*

American Medical Association. Their literature review compared the diagnoses, inheritance, response to treatment, and relapse seen in addiction to that of Type 2 diabetes mellitus, hypertension, and asthma.

Genetic factors, personal choice, and environmental factors are comparably involved in the cause and course of all these disorders. Addiction produces significant and lasting changes in brain chemistry and function. Effective medications are available for treating nicotine, alcohol, and opiate addiction, but not stimulant or marijuana dependence. Medication adherence and relapse rates are similar across these illnesses. Addiction has often been treated as if it were an acute illness. McLellan suggests that long-term care strategies of medication management and continued monitoring produce lasting benefits. They conclude that addiction should be insured, treated, and evaluated like any other chronic illness.

The authors end their report with a section listing the implications of their study. First, they recommended that as part of medical school and residency training, primary care physicians should be taught the following: addiction screening, diagnosis, brief interventions, medication management, and referral criteria that can routinely be incorporated into clinical practice.

Next, they recommend that those who write healthcare policy support recent changes in health insurance laws that require equal coverage for addiction as for other diseases. Like other chronic illnesses, the effects of addiction treatments are most effective when patients remain in continuing care and are monitored as long as it is medically necessary. Although it is unknown whether care delivered in a specialty program or coordinated through primary care will provide the maximal benefits for patients and society, it is important that practitioners adapt the care and medical monitoring strategies currently used in the treatment of other chronic illnesses to the treatment of drug dependence.

• **You not only treat the symptoms of the disease of addiction, but also train patients in coping skills to help them remain sober. Will you explain your treatments?**

Addiction is a biological, psychological, social, and spiritual illness. Treating addiction in isolation is bound to fail. In our practice, we treat the full spectrum, not just the biological. The **biological care** involves detoxification and sobriety maintenance. The **social aspects** involve creating new social networks, restoring the family social relations, life skills coaching, and training. **Recovery** requires people to respond to a series of identifiable situations that have been linked to relapse.

Two important examples are interaction with past associates who are drug and alcohol users, and responding to interpersonal stress that occurs on the job or at home. The skills training and counseling helps the recovering person manage these situations without resorting to drugs or alcohol.

• **Since you treat addiction as a disease, what is the difference in your success rates?**

Addiction is a lifelong illness, so "survival rate" is a more appropriate term. In breast cancer, we look at five-year survival rates. Similarly, in addiction we look at survival rates of sobriety. This is just one aspect of care. We also have to look at the quality of life, as with any chronic illness, addiction involves periods of remission followed by relapse.

• **I understand there are non-toxic medications that can be used to treat addiction. What are these medications, and are they available from medical doctors in regular practice?**

Addiction treatment involves two components. One is

withdrawal management and the other is sobriety maintenance. Withdrawal management can be done with "like drugs," such as methadone or Suboxone, and appropriately weaning the drug. Alternatively, the provider may let the withdrawal syndrome manifest itself and treat the symptom clusters with non-addictive medications—this second route is what I follow for withdrawal management. To contrast it with the laborious detoxification processes, we now term it "de-addiction."

Similarly, sobriety maintenance can be achieved with narcotic replacement therapies such as methadone or Suboxone, or by blocking the cravings which usually result in relapses with antagonist medications such as naltrexone and Campral, which are non-addictive.

• **I'm aware of methadone clinics which treat heroin addicts. I know that some addicts are on methadone for the rest of their lives. Is methadone still widely used in treatment?**

Addiction is a disease that primarily manifests in young adults, so in my practice I would not place an adolescent or young adult on a potentially dangerous narcotic for an indefinite period of time because the neural circuitry they created during their substance abuse can be reversed over time with sobriety, life changes, and counseling.

However, for the older addict whose brain is not as resilient as those in their teens, twenties, or thirties, methadone might be the most functional and feasible option.

While the Preventive Medicine Associates clinics do not prescribe methadone or use it in our facilities, it is still a widely used treatment. Research has demonstrated that methadone maintenance is an effective treatment for heroin and other opiate addictions. It has the benefits of reducing the use of illegal substances, being an opiate that is dispensed and monitored by a physician, diminishing needle sharing and the associated resulting complications, reducing suicidal tendencies, and decreasing the risk of drug overdose.

- **Many addicts are afraid of treatment. Should they be worried about going "cold turkey?"**

I would never recommend that a patient go "cold turkey." While a patient cannot die from withdrawal of narcotics or stimulants, withdrawal can be highly dangerous and, in the case of alcohol and benzodiazepine abuse, if detoxification is not monitored carefully by a physician, the patient could die. While our method of treatment does not utilize narcotics like methadone or buprenorphine to taper the patient off slowly or prescribe these narcotics to minimize withdrawal symptoms, our treatment is not "cold turkey." We provide our patients with simple primary care medications, treating the symptoms of the withdrawal safely and relieving much of the patients' discomfort.

Each patient experiences withdrawal differently. Some experience insomnia and anxiety, others feel pain and fatigue. While some patients suffer from constipation, others endure the opposite. They may experience excessive sweating or have a fever and not be able to sweat. Withdrawal is like the flu, only much worse, and no matter what symptoms the patient experiences, it is painful, terrifying, and unforgettable. Many patients try to detoxify themselves or prove that they are not dependent on the substance before entering treatment, and their attempt to go "cold turkey" is what enables them to realize they need help and come to us for care.

- **Once a patient becomes sober, how do they maintain their sobriety?**

Becoming sober involves far more than just physically detoxifying from the substance(s) of abuse. It requires a complete restructuring of one's everyday existence and a full commitment to this new lifestyle. This change is easier said than done. Addiction is a disease that evolves over time as the individual relies more and more on the substance and the drug becomes further ingrained in his or her life. The people one associates with while on drugs, crisis situations, times of pain, and places where one purchased or used drugs all serve as triggers for relapse once one is in recovery. Our treatment helps to educate the patient on how to avoid such triggers and cope in healthy, effective ways. For youth, there are even sober colleges, which are safe havens. Ultimately, time is the healer, and any individual who sobers up needs a meticulous life plan which he or she lives 24-hours a day. Acceptance of this reality is the key to sustained sobriety.

- **Do you recommend or work with 12-step programs?**

I tell my patients that they should go to Alcoholics Anonymous (AA) or other 12-step programs such as Narcotics Anonymous (NA). The principles of AA are the principles of a good life: being honest, being forthright, and making amends when you hurt someone. These principles prompt commonalities of trust in every society. While many people have used AA as a primary treatment, we recommend it as a key addition to primary treatment and a source of social and moral support for recovery during primary treatment and long-term recovery.

☼ **Fresh Start** ☼

Celebrity Rehab

Interview with Sherry Gaba, LCSW, Psychotherapist and Life Coach

Author of "The Law of Sobriety: Attracting Positive Energy for a Powerful Recovery"

• **Sherry, I understand you are a therapist and a life coach. You also work with Dr. Drew on VH1 Celebrity Rehab. I imagine most of the celebrities who appear on this show are crying out for help. Friends and family can usually see when their loved ones are headed for trouble. Can you explain briefly what brings people to the point where they really want help?**

People seek help when they have hit bottom, with consequences like homelessness, losing their job, spouse, or children. Their families give them an ultimatum—they have one more chance to get help. Their lives are unmanageable. Some celebrities don't hit bottom financially, so it's harder for them to get help.

• **What makes you able to offer them a hand up?**

I am a Licensed Clinical Social Worker; I work at several Malibu rehabs. I've been in 12-step programs and have personal and professional experience with recovery.

• **Is it much harder for the celebrities to seek help?**

What's hard is the fact that they have too many 'yes' people who give them drugs. They need to get those people out of their lives and get good people in. There isn't much difference between the celebrities and everyone else. They have lower self-esteem than most people think, and bigger egos. Everything is on a grander scale. People use them for their money. They also have so many people to take care of financially. Often, their extended family depends on their financial help.

• **What lead you to your profession as a life coach and therapist?**

When I was a single mom, so many people helped me that I wanted to help others. I wanted to give back. I have worked in Hospice, custody work, and with single parents. I went back to school with the intention of working with single parents, but I was able to do much more and that has been a bonus to me.

• **How successful is the program which is designed for celebrities?**

On Celebrity Rehab the celebrities work hard. They attend group therapy, 12-step programs, and they learn how to have sober fun. If they don't get it the first time, a seed has been planted. I'm there to help Dr. Drew and I also work behind the scenes of the show.

• **We all see headlines and hear news of celebrities being arrested, being drunk and disorderly, and seeking rehab. It would be nice to hear about the celebrities who are taking a stand against drugs. Can you tell stories of hope and encouragement in this direction?**

The healing aspects don't get shown, unfortunately. The media is looking for drama.

• **When you go home at night, do you have a hard time getting these problems off your mind?**

No, you learn professionally how to put it aside. It's important for me to eat right, do meditation, and exercise. I often get away for the weekend. I work on me. If I'm not okay, I can't help others.

• **What would you recommend to those who are struggling with**

addiction?

Seek help through inpatient or outpatient therapy. If you have a family member with an abuse problem, seek your own help through Al-Anon and get support through an interventionist. It can be through your church or an attorney. Get together and approach the addict with a plan. You can hire someone. An interventionist is not emotionally involved.

• **When you find a patient who responds well to treatment, what do you recommend for their continued sobriety?**

They need a good after-care program. A 12-step program is good because they will have support and have a sponsor. It's important to set up an outpatient program. Have all appointments set up before the patient is discharged from an inpatient program.

• **Have you seen success with 12-step programs?**

12-step programs are the most effective treatment because you will be around other people who understand where you are and where you've been. The patient is not isolated, and it's best that the patient is not alone. Some patients don't believe in a higher power, and some won't go to these programs. I don't force people. I work with them right where they are.

• **Do you think it is often peer pressure that leads kids to drugs? Or is there an underlying problem that needs to be worked through?**

There could be several factors: peer pressure, mental Illness, anxiety, low self esteem, family drug use, abuse, or going with the wrong crowd.

• **Do addicts need to move to another city, change their phone number, or find a whole new group of friends in order to stay away from drugs/alcohol? Or are they taught skills that will sustain them when they return to the real world?**

Moving won't help an addict—drugs will always follow. If they aren't ready to give it up, they will find drugs anywhere they go. It is helpful to change friends and lose the numbers of old friends. This is where 12-step programs really help, because the people not only understand the addiction, they are working on being sober as well. Nothing works if they aren't ready. It's much harder to change when you're a celebrity. Sometimes people need other options. I wrote my book, "The Law of Sobriety", so I could offer another option if the individual struggling with addiction is not receptive to a 12-step program.

☼ Know You Can ☼

My Rehab Experience
by Dillon - age 18

I was in junior high when my friend Riley gave me a small bag of weed. I decided to smoke it at school. I told a kid that I had it, and he told on me. I quickly handed the weed to another kid, who flushed it down the toilet. Even though I no longer had the weed, I had to stay in the office for five hours. When the principal questioned me, I kept denying that I had weed. But, finally I admitted it, because I just wanted to go home.

I was suspended from school for two weeks and sent to court. The judge sent me to DT, detention. That was the beginning of my probation.

The next time I was in trouble for taking my mom's B12 pills to school. Someone told a teacher I had marijuana pills. I was sent to outpatient drug treatment and put on probation for two weeks. During my probation, I popped some of my mom's Klonopin pills she uses for anxiety. While on the pills, I made fireworks out of a bottle rocket and it lifted off the ground and landed under a minivan. My dad tried to confront me, so I hit him in the head with a crutch. I knew I was in trouble, so I ran down the street and ended up at my aunt's house, three miles away.

I was required to report to the drug program daily. When I didn't report for several days, I was charged with AWOL, along with assault for hitting my dad, a distribution charge for giving out B12, and destruction of property. Since I ran to my cousin Brian's house, I was ordered by the court to have no contact with my aunt or cousins. This was very hard for the whole family, because we couldn't even be together for holidays.

I went to DT for thirty days, locked up in a brick room with a metal door, a thin blanket, a thin mattress, a metal toilet, and a metal sink. The bed was like sleeping on cement. When I got bored, I counted bricks. On Fridays, we watched a movie. We could only leave the room for breakfast, lunch, dinner, showers, church, and school.

Everyone in DT is dressed in used underwear, Barker brand pants, and an orange shirt. Barker makes all the clothes for DT.

After thirty days of boredom, I went to O and A, Observation and Assessment. This is like being locked up and doing community service projects for forty-five days. The state took custody of me and charged my mom child support during the time I was gone. I had to earn visitations and I got to see my mom on weekends. Once I got to see my sister and both sets of grandparents for about thirty minutes. When my sentence was over, custody was given back to my mom. I was sent to ASAP, Adolescent Substance Abuse Program. This is a day treatment program. I went home at night. I was in that program for six months until I got kicked out for selling

Ecstasy.

My mom was very frustrated, but she registered me in regular school. I went back to school for a few days before breaking my probation again. I didn't go home and didn't check in with my mom or my probation officer. When I talked to my mom a few days later, she told me I had a warrant out for my arrest. I really didn't want to get locked up again, so I went on the run. I was high and lived at my girlfriend's house for two weeks. I spent Thanksgiving with my girlfriend. My mom knew where I was, but she was waiting for me to turn myself in. I wanted to get everything over with before Christmas, so I turned myself in, thinking I'd only be in DT for a couple days. The reality hit me harder than a smack.

I spent the night in DT and the next day my probation officer came to visit me and give me a drug test. I failed for cocaine, weed, and Ecstasy. I had court the day after that and my judge made a no-contact order with my girlfriend and that really pissed me off. He sentenced me to thirty days in DT and sixty days at Journey Impact Ranch.

I spent Christmas and New Year's in DT! I was pissed because I'd rather be around my family than a bunch of dudes who were locked up.

Journey Impact Ranch is in Mona, Utah. I was sentenced there for sixty days in the coldest part of the winter. The Journey program helped me realize a lot of things and it had a big impact on my life.

My hair was long, below my shoulders, before I went to Journey. I got mad when they told me I had to have my head shaved. I was told that I would fail the program if I didn't cut my hair and I'd go back to DT, so I let them shave it off.

There were thirty boys and a bunch of staff members at the

ranch. We slept in a yurt for two weeks in January. It had a wood platform with a tarp covering the top. Each yurt had three bunk beds. It was so cold I couldn't sleep. We had to study and do assignments to earn better sleeping arrangements.

While I was there, I watered and fed horses, cows, chickens, goats, and llamas, and I also milked cows every morning and every night. It was so cold to get up in the morning and my feet were frozen.

The wilderness trek was also part of the Journey experience. Two leaders took eight boys at a time to the wilderness for six days.

When the sun came up, we would start hiking. Since the frost got our stuff wet, we had to walk barefoot until our shoes dried. Our feet were always cold. We continued to hike until the sun went down and we would set up camp, eat, and have social development group. This group really made me think about a lot about stuff. We talked about our feelings, and did exercises to make us realize what we had done to hurt the people in our lives.

We slept in sleeping bags on top of the snow, with a tarp under us, and no tent. Each of us had an eight-foot long living area and couldn't leave that space at night.

During the wilderness trek, we had to climb huge rock mountains carrying sixty-pound backpacks. It took us all day to get to the top. It was extremely hard and physically exhausting, but it was worth it. I felt so accomplished when we were at the top. It was the best feeling I have ever felt. It was a better high than any drug I have ever tried.

The Journey program took a lot of effort to complete, but I felt like a new person when I got out. I feel bad for all I put my mom through, because she had to pay money out of her pocket for me while I was in JJS custody, and she had to pay for my treatment and drug testing. I also put my parents through so much worry when I ran away, got locked up and failed my drug tests. I'm so sorry that I fought with my dad, took drugs to school, and damaged other people's property. I wish I could fix all the problems I've caused, but the best I can do is to prove I'm doing better now.

What did you learn?
- Drugs aren't worth it; they ruin a lot of things.
- I realize how I treated my family and what I put them through wasn't right.
- I hope other kids don't have to go as far as I did to learn the lessons I had to learn.

What do you have to do to stay off drugs?
- Not hang around certain friends.
- Go to AA meetings, because people there help me.
- Go to church.
- Hang around my family more, but not my cousin and his girlfriend.

☼ START OVER FRESH ☼

TREATING THE REAL PROBLEM
by Kristen Moeller
Author of "Waiting for Jack"

I began drinking in junior high
EARLY DECISIONS

Small things can set us off —tiny incidents that matter to no one else but loom large in our minds. We latch onto them, magnify them, and they become indelible, forming who we become. Even though these events may have occurred long ago, we get messages, learn lessons, and make decisions that impact our feelings, thinking, and behavior. When we make these formative decisions, we are not always aware that we alter the course of our lives.

One of these moments happened in the third grade. While reading out loud, I said, "the windy city is known as 'Chick-a-go'..." (instead of Chicago) and the class erupted in laughter. I plopped down in complete humiliation. Another time, I brought the "wrong" present to a birthday party—instead of an action figure, the birthday boy was to receive a fairy doll. Making mistakes—especially in front of my peers—was painful. I avoided it at all costs.

Later, when my parents divorced, I irrationally thought I might have prevented the split if I had only known or if I'd been a better kid. I began to interpret these things as, "Something is wrong with me."

In seventh grade, I found a "solution" when I discovered alcohol. Drinking provided a new kind of confidence and freedom. For that moment, life looked rosy.

FAILING TO GET IT RIGHT

Even with this new way to avoid my problems, I was shy and struggled to fit in as I moved back and forth between my mom in Florida and my dad in Massachusetts. It seemed that with each new school and group of kids, I could never quite get my outfit right. What was very popular at one school was not cool at the other.

Therefore, I delighted in the discovery of recreational drugs—I joined other kids with similar avoidance issues and found a social group where I fit in. Some mornings we snorted coke in the school parking lot. Or we would spend our lunch hour drinking at a local restaurant or doing lines at the drug dealer's house.

As cool as this felt, the realities of life could not be ignored entirely. At home, my mother drank to cope with her losses, and both she and my brother always seemed sad. I craved support and understanding and had no idea how to get it. Feeling utterly alone, I once told my father, "I wish something was wrong with me so people would pay attention to me."

SOMETHING WRONG WITH ME

When I looked in the mirror, I didn't see the cute, slender blonde everyone else saw. I thought my thighs weren't right, my nose was too big and my lips too small, and I was sure my legs were too short. All this external focus covered up the deep internal insecurities I had no idea how to address, which lead to the illogical conclusion that I needed to lose weight. I began restricting my food. When people asked, "Have you lost weight?" I heard, "You look great!" Ah, I got the attention I had craved!

Later that year, I got the flu and threw up for three days straight. After the vomiting subsided, I stepped on the scale. Delighted to see how the weight had melted away, something shifted for me.

I began vomiting my food whenever I felt slightly uncomfortable with what I had eaten. I believed I could handle it, but it wasn't long before I realized it had me. I couldn't stop. I grew increasingly frail and thin. Even I eventually noticed. My concerned friends lovingly fed me my favorite foods to help me grow stronger. This was the attention I had been waiting for.

Unknowingly, I had become bulimic.

COLLEGE LIFE

I moved to Boulder, Colorado to attend college. Although I was able to hide my eating disorder, even with my gaunt frame and strange eating habits, there was no need to hide my alcohol and drug use. It seemed everyone liked to party. After the local bars closed for the night, we'd either stay up for hours snorting lines of coke, or I'd find an excuse to ditch my friends and drive around aimlessly in the dark, binge-eating.

Desperate to find a place to purge, I often resorted to the bathroom at Dunkin Donuts at three in the morning, or sometimes I threw up in garbage bags in my car.

Once I passed out, parked on the side of a deserted mountain road. I woke up to find a garbage bag heavy with vomit sitting on the seat next to me. With feelings of self-loathing, shame, and disgust, I quietly crept back to my sorority house, swearing and promising myself I'd never do it again.

The next day, I did it again.

My infrequent visits to my eternally supportive therapist kept me alive. She tried everything: anti-depressants from A to Z, hypnosis, and a food journal. When I realized I couldn't drink while taking one of the anti-depressants, I turned to smoking pot. I didn't enjoy it as much, but it helped ease my growing angst.

One afternoon while driving home from one of my rare sanctuaries, the tanning bed, I smoked a joint. When I got out of the car, I felt strange. I made it up the stairs to my room before my eyes rolled back into my head, and I collapsed with a seizure. Observing this event, my roommate had had enough—she called my parents.

Also on their final straw, my parents called an emergency meeting with my therapist. A plan was placed before me. I had two weeks to "straighten up" or I would be put into a treatment center immediately. Either way, it was emphasized, I was going to treatment—my only choice was when.

Being wrenched from school would be the ultimate humiliation, so I pulled it together, cut back on drugs, and did better with my food, which meant I starved myself to avoid vomiting. I kept a food journal that read something like "Monday: apple with peanut butter, bagel, and Diet Coke." I felt proud—no vomiting, and look at that self-control!

GETTING TREATMENT

After school ended for the summer, I went to my first treatment center. I learned that "fat" is not actually a feeling. When I felt fat, I learned to look beneath the surface to what might really be going on. This gave me the opportunity to express some of the deep emotions I usually shoved down with food and then vomited back up. I learned about assertiveness and how to say, "When you said my designer jeans were tacky, that hurt my feelings." (I still wasn't brave enough to say this to anyone, but at least I knew how.)

I absorbed as much as I could and followed the suggestions. I returned to college with hope for my future. For a while I used my new tools and felt strong. But returning to the same party-filled environment, I fell back into my old patterns. I felt even more ashamed of my binging and purging behavior. Now that my roommate knew why I hid for so long in the bathroom, it was much harder to hide what I was doing.

During my final months of college, I felt the buzz of excitement among my friends and classmates as they prepared to begin their new careers, but I was terrified. All I could feel was dread. I grew desperate. I hated myself and my life. "What now?" I thought. "I can't do anything!"

One particularly gloomy day while wandering aimlessly through the mall during a binge, I glanced at a vacant wall and imagined a vision of a black hole. I realized I was afraid to feel my feelings and was terrified I would be lost in this black hole forever. All my life I had avoided pain as best I could, but now I knew I had actually caused myself more pain by doing so. In that moment at the mall, I was ready for a solution, and I was willing to change.

Aware of my despair, my parents stepped in for the second time. My mom, sober since 1987, proposed a 12-step-based treatment center. This time I knew I was ready—I had waited long enough. The night before treatment seemed the longest of my life. My anxiety was intense, but my willingness to change carried me through. Then on my second day in treatment, when the counselor told me I was not only to give up my bulimic practices but alcohol and drugs as well, I was afraid. I called my father and begged him to come get me. "I think you should stay," he said firmly.

That was September 25, 1989, and I chose to stay. My life changed forever on that day.

☼ **Love Yourself** ☼

Treating the Rehab Doctor
Dr. Talia Witkowski - age 29

I became addicted at age 14.

Addictions: Food, fantasy and imagination which led to drug and alcohol abuse, lying, manipulation of others, and self-destructive behaviors.

I grew up going to Jewish day school all the way up to ninth grade. Both of my parents were drug addicts. I didn't find out about my parents' drug use until I was in high school.

While I was growing up, I always needed more love. No amount of love I got from anyone ever felt like enough. I used overeating and masturbation to get by emotionally before I found alcohol and drugs.

I did well in the strict environment of the private school, but when my parents sent me to public school, in the ninth grade,

I began drinking to fit in. I went through ninth grade in a fog from drinking so much. It gave me great pride to binge drink and never pass out or throw up. I out-drank most of the guys. I also smoked pot once or twice and tried a quarter of a tab of acid, just to fit in.

I often overheard my parents discussing my behavior. This worried me, but didn't make a difference to my social activities. Fearing the worst if I continued with the same group of friends, they sent me to boarding school.

At this school, I was the only white, Jewish girl sitting at the black table. Because my black friends didn't do drugs or drink, I didn't either. Rather than using drugs, I began having sex with black boys. Among this group, rather than being over overweight I was considered "curvaceous and sexy."

I went through a culture change in college, attending Brandeis University, which is 60-80% Jewish. Amazingly, I kept my grades up, even though I smoked pot almost daily for eight years, starting my freshman year of college. My pride in handling alcohol continued with binge drinking throughout college. I also took magic mushrooms and tried cocaine, even after my dad, who had been addicted, warned me not to. I didn't love it, thank God.

My favorite high was the combination of alcohol and pot. By taking the two, I was able to temporarily curb my appetite for food. At the end of the night, however, I would overeat as a result of starving myself all day.

After college, I went to grad school and became a therapist, specializing in eating disorders and addictions. I was living a lie. I worked with people in treatment centers and private practice by day, and went home to use drugs at night. Depending on which extreme I was on at the time, I would either overeat or try to control my weight with diet and exercise. I would also binge drink and/or smoke pot and usually find my way to a club or bar to feed the sex/love addiction.

On a spiritual retreat one summer, I met a guy from London. I fell into an "obsession" with him. We kept in contact through phone calls and e-mail and eventually started dating over the phone. One day he said he loved me, but wasn't attracted to me because of the size of my body. I was devastated, desperate, and wanted to do anything to win him back.

I became vegan, ate healthy, and lost the weight. I went to as many as three yoga classes a day, trying to shed the pounds. I would still do some drugs and binge drink occasionally, but was trying to be a "good girl" and get clean to try and impress him.

With my new healthy body, I eventually visited London to try to get the guy back. We got drunk the first night and ended up having unprotected sex, shamefully realizing I wanted to get pregnant to win him back.

Although I was clean from drugs and alcohol before I went to visit him, I was only living so clean because I had substituted my substance addiction for addition to this man.

When his friend gave us Ecstasy, I took it because I wanted to impress him and make him like me. I was insane. Here I was, an addiction doctor in the middle of a London ghetto, taking Ecstasy and going to raves. We didn't sleep for what felt like days. It was awful. I was hurting myself trying to get this man's attention and love, but the more I sold my soul, the less he wanted me. I even asked him to marry me.

He said, "No, can't we just have fun?" I was heartbroken.

I went home very depressed and visited my friends from college. On my birthday, December 30th, I started drinking and smoking pot. He text-messaged me on my birthday but didn't call or email on New Year's. I was so angry and hurt.

I can see now that I wanted to kill myself and didn't care what I put inside of me—I just wanted to feel good, or not feel at all. I did cocaine, smoked lots of pot, and drank all I could to try to escape the pain inside. It didn't work.

I eventually took the whole bag of cocaine my friend had and went to the bathroom with it. I couldn't get high enough and nearly overdosed. The next thing I knew, I was in a limo, throwing up over and over again. It's a good thing I threw up, because I probably would have died. But I woke up the next day and started again, smoking and drinking.

My finances were so messed up as a result of the life I was living. I was a liar and a con artist, but it was because I was in a lot of pain emotionally and didn't have a way out. I was supposed to be the expert, for crying out loud!

During this time, I was still mourning the guy from London. One day I even got on my knees and prayed. I promised that I would do anything if God would let me have him back. I'm not religious and besides, Jews don't pray on their knees. I was raised to pray standing as a sign of respect to God.

Soon after, I had a patient who was being sent to a hospital for bulimia, but her mom didn't want her to go. She had heard of a program called *Heal Your Hunger* (www.healyourhunger.com), which was supposed to be a last resort. She asked me to use my rapport with her daughter to make the introduction. I was interested in making money, so I set up the meeting. By helping my patient, I met Roy Nelson, and he became my mentor.

I was hurting bad and Roy helped me. I was dependant on every type of substance imaginable, including drugs, alcohol, caffeine, and tobacco. I talked about the guy from London and the pain

I was in. I cried and the pain was gone, lifted. Roy isn't a therapist; he's just a man who hit bottom and nothing would work for him. He learned a way to live that allowed him to be clean, sober and thin (without having to diet or exercise) and simply teaches others to live this way if they so desire. I desired. The best part about this program was that unlike every other time I had gotten clean, I actually enjoyed life and didn't want to shoot myself in the head from the boredom or the longing for the drugs or alcohol or my "old life." This program was different because it worked where all else failed.... and I didn't even need to go into a treatment center.

I started treating the real problem, which stems from that feeling of not being good enough and not being able to get enough love. I went from feeling inadequate to feeling better than I had felt my whole life.

Heal Your Hunger helped me through a very simple living program consisting of mediation, writing exercises, and other tools of recovery specific to this program.

I also needed a mentor, and continue to talk to Roy to this day. With each passing day, my life gets better and better. I lost all the excess weight I once carried (60 lbs) and have kept it off for two years. I have also been free, sober, healthy, and happy for all that time. They give you the 'armor' you need to live without addictions and eating disorders.

I share my story because I think if it's the right thing for someone; it will help them have hope. *Heal the Hunger* is the only way I could get help and change my life. I am a therapist, I have friends who are therapists and I have studied from some very special spiritual leaders, but none of them could help me. This is special and may work for you when all other forms of recovery do not.

I hope this is helpful for you.

Sincerely,
Dr. Talia Witkowski

☼ Courage to Get Well ☼

Digging My Way Out
by Kevin Haushultz

Kevin is also the author of "I Crossed the Line" in the Cocaine section

I returned home after graduating from college with a serious cocaine addiction. However, powdered cocaine wasn't easily accessible in Hartford, Connecticut. I quickly discovered that I could get a bag of heroin for $10, a fraction of my daily cocaine habit. I instantly fell in love with the effects of heroin, and was shooting the drug within a week. I had a series of three overdoses, all nearly fatal.

I tried outpatient treatment at a local facility, which didn't help me much because I wasn't ready to stop my habit. I relapsed by drinking a few beers, and later on that night, I had returned to Hartford to get my drug of choice. I tried to run away from my problems for a few more months, until I had another overdose. At that point, my parents took me to my psychiatrist, who told me about Suboxone, a new treatment option for opiate addicts. I decided to give it a try, as if I didn't, I would be faced with living on the streets of Hartford rather than at my parents' home. I maintained on Suboxone for a little over a year. Although I wasn't using heroin, I continued to exhibit the same behaviors. I stopped attending 12-step meetings, and only attended relapse prevention classes occasionally.

I once again attempted to drink "socially," and once again, reverted back to heroin. At this point, my parents informed me that I needed to go to an inpatient facility. Reluctantly, I attended a rehab center in the northwest corner of Connecticut. I met a number of individuals who really took me "under their wing", and for the first time in years, I was actually able to feel emotions again. Although I still had feelings of shame and guilt about my addiction, I felt welcomed and comfortable around the other clients and staff in this rehabilitation center.

During my stay, one of the suggestions made was to go on to a halfway house. At that point, I did want to stay in recovery, but wasn't sure that my addiction had taken me to such depths that I needed to go to a halfway house. I definitely wanted to return to the comforts of home, however, I decided to give it a shot. Luckily, I decided to stick it out, and that halfway house is where I really discovered the joys of recovery. I attended my first sober dance and laughed harder than I had in years, and really formed a connection with some of my housemates. I attended a Recovery Walk in Hartford, where I discovered that there were thousands of people in recovery in Connecticut and I didn't need to be ashamed of it. I also discovered that there was a way to have fun without drugs and that it wasn't just about going to meetings—it was about a new way of life.

My girlfriend knew one of the staff members of CCAR (Connecticut Community for Addiction Recovery), and she thought it might be fun to get involved with the organization. I attended a chapter meeting at one of their local Recovery Community Centers in Hartford, and had a deep appreciation for the organization's values—to help put a positive face on recovery and remove some of the associated barriers. I began to volunteer with them and learned how to be a trainer through the organization. In August of 2007, a position was posted for a Telephone Recovery Support Coordinator to help run a program in which volunteers called a person in recovery once a week just to check in and see how they were doing. I applied for the position and got it. Now, two and a half years later, I am running the program for the state, and have even done technical assistance in other states to show them how to implement a Telephone Recovery Support program for their Recovery Community. I am back in school, going for my Masters in Social Work, and recently received my Associate's in Drug and Alcohol Recovery Counseling. I purchased a home in 2008, something I never would have imagined just 4 years ago. My life today is truly beyond my wildest dreams.

☼ **ENCOURAGE OTHERS** ☼

Alateen
by Savanna Peterson

Alateen is a 12-Step program for teenage children of alcoholics and drug addicts. Before I went to Alateen, I thought no one had a family like mine and no one suffers like I do. No one else has to go through the stuff I go through every night.

I found out about Alateen through my grandma. We were already writing our book together and Grandma thought this group would help me with my family situation. She told me we were going to the meetings for research. I also went because Mom drinks and Dad is an addict and he has never been around. When I went there, I thought, Wow! There are other people out there with the same problems. The best part is hearing people say the things I think and have to go through and learning how to handle it. I felt so good when I walked out of the first meeting. The leaders don't always make you feel welcome—like when my cousin and I burst out laughing for no reason—but the teenagers do.

SOBER COLLEGES
Princeton Review's top 10 list
'Stone Cold' Sober Colleges

1. Brigham Young University
2. Wheaton College
3. College of the Ozarks
4. Grove City College
5. U.S. Naval Academy
6. U.S. Coast Guard Academy
7. U.S. Air Force Academy
8. Queens College
9. Wellesley College
10. Calvin College

Additional Information:

Woodbury University in Burbank, California.

West Hills, California

Robert "Rob" Gilson, CTC - Admissions Director

800-336-0053

www.sobercollege.com

This Sober College—focuses on getting sober; starting a career or college education for ages 17-26. This is a combined rehab and college experience while working with the campus of

Gateway College Campus

Requires six months sobriety to attend

www.gatewaycollegecampus.com

14. Taking a Stand Against Drugs

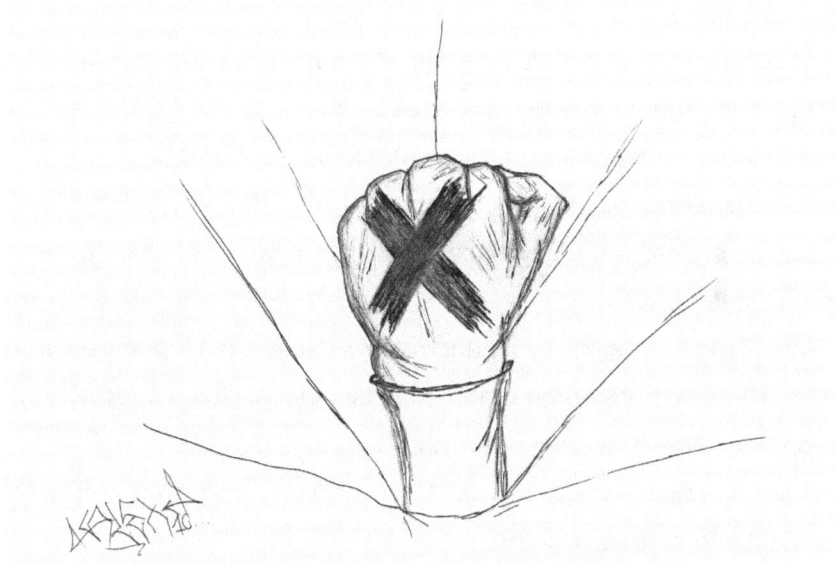

☼ Be Alert ☼
Times to be on Guard for Drugs and Alcohol
by Jill Vanderwood

- **Holiday Celebrations**—in some families, holidays are celebrated with wine, champagne, or beer.
- **Spring Break**—when kids go away for spring break, they are usually celebrating a break from school—and a break from parents, which will likely include drugs/alcohol and binge drinking.
- **Graduation**—this is a big night of celebrating. If nothing is planned

ahead, you could likely fall into a situation with alcohol and even end up riding with a drunk driver.

• **Family Reunions**—yes, it's the only time I'm ever faced with alcohol and drugs. Since young teens and adults who have not used, or haven't used for years, are faced with a situation where they look up to certain family members, they are forced to make an uncomfortable decision.

• **Meeting Up with Old Friends**—"What happened to you? You used to be fun. Come on and have a drink with me." Old friend reunions are often planned around drinking or pot smoking.

• **Old Drinking or Druggy Friends**—these long-forgotten friends from your past will likely show up at your home or your parents' home looking for you.

• **Weddings**—the spiked punch bowl usually isn't guarded from kids. Relatives may offer drinks to kids, saying, "It's a special occasion", or "One little drink won't hurt him."

• **Family Trips**—some travelers are nervous and drink too much while flying across country.

• **After School Visits with Friends**—going home with a friend can sometimes involve unguarded bottles of wine/hard liquor. Also, kids may find their parents' stash of marijuana or prescription drugs.

• **Sleepovers**—at a slumber party, kids could get into wine/alcohol or other substances if they aren't monitored.

• **Movies**—in movies, alcohol is shown as sophisticated or fun; a couple having a drink over dinner is portrayed as natural. Showing drunken people is used as humor, or those who are drinking seem to be popular or the life of the party. What they don't usually show is a drinker vomiting into the toilet afterward.

• **Be Guarded**—either be prepared to say 'no' or hang around people you know won't pressure you to drink or do drugs.

☼ **Believe in Yourself** ☼

What is Expected?
by Savanna Peterson

• If you grow up in a large family, it is expected that you can't afford college. You may get bad grades, knowing that college isn't even an option. Are there other options for you?

Yes! You can try your best. Get the best grades possible so you can get a scholarship. You can live above the expectations of others. If you have a job, you can save your money for college. Find your talents and use them to help you get to where you want to be in life. Many people get a scholarship for musical or athletic talents.

• If your parents are professors, you may be expected to go to the best colleges and go into the family business. This may also be your plan, but if not, don't give up. You have the power to do anything you want.

• If you grow up in the ghetto, society expects you to wear hand-me-down clothes and have head lice. It is also expected that you won't succeed in life. Don't do what is expected—become anyone you want to be. Dream of the life you want.

I Won't Be What People Expect Me to Be

In junior high, my older brother started hanging around kids who skipped school, and he didn't try to get good grades. He began drinking and smoking weed with his friends.

I am four years younger than my brother. When I got to junior high, the teachers didn't expect very much from me. They thought I would fail math, but I showed them that I could do well. The principal expected me to be a troublemaker, but I was never sent to the principal's office.

When my mom went to work, my brother had parties with his friends. My granddad was there, but he was usually drinking and couldn't do anything. The parties were usually on weekends, and I would stay at my friends' houses to get away from it, but sometimes they partied on weeknights, as well. During these times, I would either stay in my room or call Grandma to pick me up.

One, day I was waiting for my friend to come to my house to sleep over. Her dad was about to drop her off in front of my house. She got out of the car, and then he said, "Wait, is this where your friend lives?"

"Yes. Bye, I love you, Dad."

"Get back in the car now! You are never to speak to this girl again."

Her dad was a cop and he said they had been watching my house for quite a while. They never had a search warrant, so they just watched and waited outside, trying to pull someone over for DUI.

When someone would call the cops about my brother's parties, they couldn't do anything unless someone let them into the house, or they could see drugs or alcohol from the door.

The girl called me that night to tell me what her dad said. After that she wouldn't even talk to me at school. She began spreading rumors about me, and that really hurt. About a year later, she came up to me and asked if my brother could get her some weed.

When I see my brother's friends, they ask me to sell them some weed, or say, "are you rolling?"

I won't be what they expect me to be! My main goal is to make sure I grow up to be somebody, to avoid drugs and alcohol, and to make sure my little sister stays away from drugs and alcohol.

☼ **KNOW YOURSELF** ☼

CHEERLEADING
by Rebecca Kanefsky

Other stories by Rebecca include: "Disneyland", and "The Coke Man"

My dad is Jewish and my mother is Roman Catholic. When I lived in Kentucky, we were the only Jewish family in the entire population of 10,000 people, so we really stood out. No one probably would have known, but our last name was very distinctive. Because there wasn't a Temple in the area, I started taking my younger brothers to the Baptist Church. Sundays after church, we were always the last ones to be dropped off from the church bus. The driver would take us to the store to buy groceries before dropping us off at home.

Since my dad and stepmom were the major drug dealers in the small Kentucky town where I grew up, people assumed I was a druggie, too. So, I strived to prove everyone wrong. I knew I didn't have any limitations from my parents, since they only cared when they had done too many of their own pills, and they would accuse me and my siblings of stealing them.

First, I joined the youth group at church, where I could hang out with kids my own age who had the same goals and aspirations I did. We helped each other stay away from drugs by going to parties with the buddy system.

Second, the pastor of my church knew about the serious drug problems going on around me and encouraged me to join the cheerleading squad at school. If I were caught drinking or doing drugs, I would be kicked off the squad.

During middle school, I started cheering for football and basketball games. My cheerleading continued into high school. Even though my dad wasn't very happy that I wanted to cheer, I did it anyway. He would often put obstacles in my path to divert me into quitting or making it impossible, because it was very expensive. My dad was on drugs and living on welfare, so he was never in the position to pay for anything. The pastor of my church was always looking out for me to make sure I had everything I needed to be successful. It was very embarrassing when he would stand up in church on a Sunday and ask the congregation to "be very generous today, so we can help out a little girl who needs a new cheerleading outfit for school."

As a group, the cheerleaders would host yard sales and bake sales. These were easy ways to earn money for uniforms, training camps, etc. However, this didn't cover everything. And that's when my mom and grandparents would send me money. Little did they know that I'd ask for more than I needed, since my dad would take half to three quarters of the money they sent. When I told Dad I would have to bring at least five dollars to all the away games, as well as the home games, this was a huge issue with him. Why was I entitled to five dollars every other week, when my brothers were not? He felt that he would have to provide it for them as well. I tried to convince him that I would earn the money by doing chores for our neighbor, but this didn't appease him.

In my ninth grade year, during cheer season, my dad asked me to bake him some cupcakes. He was always praising my baking skills and would dote on me when I would bake for him. I was stunned when I found two boxes of cake mix, because these items could not be purchased with food stamps. I was even more surprised that when they were done, he presented me with two cans of frosting.

After I finished baking, my dad told me to make a bake sale sign. There's a rule that we can't do any individual fundraising, unless there are at least two cheerleaders involved, so there wouldn't be any money issues. I told him that I could either be suspended or let go for doing my own fundraising, and his reply was, "You promise?"

After I baked the cupcakes and made the sign, my dad told me to get into my uniform. He took me to the only large store in our town, which was Walmart. Before he let me off in front of the store, he told me to sell the cupcakes for seventy-five cents each. I had three dozen cupcakes and when he returned to pick me up, I should have $27, no more and no less. I was stuck. If I didn't sell the cupcakes, my dad would be furious. If I did sell them, I would be kicked off the cheerleading squad. There was nowhere else for me to go, and nothing else for me to do. While I was selling the cupcakes, right out in front of the whole town, some girls on the cheerleading squad came by. They told the leader what I was doing and I was confronted on Monday at school. Of course, my dad took all the money I had earned that day to support his and my stepmom's drug habits. My cheer advisor told me I was suspended from cheerleading. I had to pay all the money I had earned that day back to the team.

I contacted my grandmother and my mother to ask for money for cheerleading. It took a whole semester before I was allowed back on the squad.

To this day, I live my life as an alcoholic. Even though I do not have a drinking problem nor have I ever, I have a very addictive personality and so does my daughter. I live and raise my daughter like we are one drink away from being alcoholics.

My dad is still the main drug dealer in our Kentucky town. I moved away when I graduated from high school. Several years later, when I went back for a high school reunion, everyone was either going into or coming out of drug rehab, and I knew my dad was responsible.

☼ **REMEMBER WHO YOU ARE** ☼

I Always Knew
An Interview with actor Tray Chaney

Author of: "The Truth You Can't BeTray"

- **Tray, you are a young man of many talents, including acting, singing and writing your own book. Did you always know you'd be a star?**

I knew I would be something in life, I truly thought I would be known for my dancing, because that's what I started out with when I was eight years old. I had no idea that I would sing, write, or act.

- **What's it like to be in the public eye?**

Being in the public eye is amazing, I have always wanted folks to recognize me even when I was a child dancing at The Apollo Theater. I use to say to myself that one day people will know who I am when I walk down the streets, and I love it to this day.

- **How did you pursue your acting career?**

When I got the role on The Wire, I enjoyed it so much and I thought it was the best thing in the world to get on TV and be recognized the next day. I wanted to do more and more with remembering scripts, so I continued to pursue my acting by taking classes with Linda Townsend Management, and ended up landing a few more roles that I treasure.

- **We hear news of stars being arrested for drugs, or going into rehab. We also see fallen stars make a comeback after several years. What's it like for you to take a stand against drugs when they are so accessible?**

Well, coming from a strong family that is against drugs 100%, it is easy for me to "just say no", and I am happy that I can do that. My parents have always told me to be a leader and not a follower, so I decided that I will not do what everyone else is doing when it comes to drugs, being on the news, going to rehab—that's just not the kind of attention I want in life.

- **Are there others in your line of work who support your drug-free decision?**

Oh, yes, there are several people I associate with who support my decision, and those are the people that I tend to be with on a regular basis.

- **Would you be where you are today if you had fallen into the trap of drug abuse?**

No, I would be nowhere near my goals if I had taken drugs! I never want to be like that and have vowed not to.

- **Have you witnessed friends who took the path of drugs and alcohol?**

Yes, I have been a witness to close friends and family members who have taken that path to abuse drugs and alcohol, and it is not a good look at all.

- **Where are they now, in relation to their dreams?**

These same folks are somewhere, strung out. I can't even understand what they are talking about half the time. If they had any dreams of being a successful person in life, it just went right out the window and they have landed themselves either in a rehab or in their graves, sad to say.

How do you avoid drugs?

One way that I personally avoid drugs is by watching my associations. I don't do drugs, so I don't go around people who use drugs. I keep my distance. And I always remember and apply the scripture in the Bible that my parents have instilled in my head, *Bad association spoils useful habits*--1 Cor. 15:33.

- **Do you have a plan in place in case/when the situation comes up?**

Yes, my plan is to just leave and get away from the situation, don't be around such bad things, and have no dealing with it.

- **Tray, I hear education was very important to you, and your parents wouldn't allow you to follow your career without your education. Why are you such an advocate of education and literacy?**

My mom and dad always said, "There's nothing like a well-educated African American man." So they always took me to the library to read books as a young person. I had to read my Bible daily, and study hard to get good grades in school. If I wasn't getting A's or B's in school, my parents were at the school, on my case. And I didn't want them coming to class with me each day, so I studied hard and got my education.

- **Have you witnessed others along the way who didn't finish school?**

Yes, there were friends who use to hang out with me who didn't finish school. They would ask me, "How do you hang out with us and get good grades?" I didn't know they were failing. I would kick it with them, but when it was time to study for a test, I was home studying my lessons, and I went all the way through school with a breeze.

- **What kind of jobs do they have now?**

Most of them don't even have a job, or they work at jobs paying minimum wage because they didn't finish school and they don't have the skills that they need to get computer jobs or jobs that require office skills like typing, faxing, copying, etc.

• **Most young people don't write an autobiography. What made you decide to be a role model and write your book?**

I wanted my fans to know how I got to be where I am today, and some of the trials I went through to get here. Also, I want the young ones to know that if they have dreams, they can follow them, become whatever it is that they want to become in life, and to never give up.

• **What advice would you give kids who would like to follow their dreams?**

I would tell them to strive hard and never give up. Don't let anyone tell you that you can't do something you are trying to do. If you work hard and stay focused, you can do anything.

• **Who has influenced you most in your career?**

My parents, mainly, but also my fans. It's is always good to know that people are watching your career and they want to see you do more because they love your work.

• **What do you do to relax or clear your mind?**

I go home to my immediate family. We get in the car and go to my parents' house and have the biggest party, laughing, dancing, playing games, and just enjoying one another all night.

• **Thank you, Tray, for being such a strong role model for others. I also want to thank you for your time and interest in Savanna's book about staying drug free.**

☼ **High Five** ☼

Radical Parenting
by Vanessa Van Petton

Vanessa is the founder of Radical Parenting and the author of "You're Grounded," which she wrote when she was 17. She is now traveling around the world to interview families for her new book, "Parenting is Flat."

She is headed to South America for five weeks to interview forty-five families. She has interns all over the world. She recently worked with Tokyo Interns to interview families in that country. The main question on her mind—Does the Internet Bring Families Closer? This book is not yet published, but the topic is showing a growing interest from people around the world.

- **Why did you decide to write your first book?**

When I was in high school, my friends were good kids. One of my friends took a downward spiral and got caught with marijuana and paraphernalia. He was sent to rehab. When I visited him in rehab, I asked why he did it. He told me, "to get back at my parents."

That's why I started writing about why teens use drugs as an escape and a tool to get back at parents.

I'm very honest with parents and kids. I don't have a counseling license. When I speak to kids who admit to drugs, I ask them to go into therapy.

- **Did You Ever Feel Pressure to Do Drugs?**

Yes, I was pressured to do drugs. I'm in my twenties and I am still pressured.

I gave my parents plenty of gray hairs, but never because of drugs. I have one older brother and two younger sisters. They are all great, and none of us have done drugs.

When I ask kids why they do drugs, most of them tell me they are bored and there was nothing better to do. It's easy to say no, but kids need something better to do. I decided it's not a choice I want to make. There are too many risks and negative consequences. If you can say "No, thank you," it helps others not as confident to say "No, thank you." Any person who would love you more if you did drugs isn't a person you would want to love you.

Kids need people to talk to besides their parents, such as cousins, teachers, counselors, and dance teachers. My dance teacher said she valued her body. She only wanted to put good, healthy food into her body. She worked too hard to get into shape, and never wanted to put drugs or harmful things into her body. That stuck with me.

Parenting is different with each child. There are highs and lows in relationships, but parents need to take the time to know the child's needs, and teens should take the time to know their parents', as well.

Prevention Solutions
Planning Activities
www.radicalparenting.com

I work with prevention solutions. Teens want to stay sober. Parents need to provide alternative activities, concerts, or movies. If you don't have a lot of money, have kids over for sports in the park. Get friends together for crafts.

Now, I am not delusional. I know that even if you provide enough fun activities for 100 weekends, teens will still find ways to drink/do drugs/have sex if they want. Yet, I do think that by helping create activities, you are:

a) Showing them you care

b) Showing them that you pay attention, so if they try anything, you will probably find out

c) Allowing less opportunity for them to be bored and create questionable activities out of boredom

d) Separating kids who will drink/smoke/have sex to rebel, no matter what, from those who simply end up trying it because it's around and there's nothing better to do. (This is totally my opinion from what I saw in high school. My group of friends and I separated from another group in 11th grade because they started drinking in a park on the weekends.)

Planning alternative activities can be important, but you don't need to do it all yourself. I think it is a great idea to get together with a group of parents from school, or all of your child's friends' parents, and make a committee to plan something each weekend and take turns carpooling, cooking, and hosting. That way, you are not responsible for everything, and all the parents can keep an eye out for suspicious behavior together. Here are 10 suggestions for activities parents can create/provide/encourage so teens have less opportunity to come up with their own…

1. Paintballing/Mini-Golf/Laser tag: Okay, this is three in one, but teens usually love doing these kinds of activities, they can be co-ed and not that much money for a few hours of amusement (and physical activity).

2. Comedy Clubs: There are a lot of improv clubs, comedy clubs, or even coffee shops that have stand-up and that allow all ages. This can be a really fun weekend night for teens. You could also ask in advance to use a local coffee shop for the teens to do their own stand-up one night, and they will all buy coffee and bring friends as an incentive for the owner.

3. Plan a Themed Party: So, this sounds lame, but I don't mean plan a themed party in the 4th grade sense. Hold an 80's movie marathon and make dinner or fondue, have a pop-culture trivia night, pool party and BBQ, or a murder mystery…

4. Dinner and a Show: There are lots of places that offer dinner and then some sort of entertainment. We used to go to a place that served Mexican food and then held a salsa class with a salsa band for all ages, or you can go to a place like Medieval Times, where they have food and then a jousting show.

5. Celebrate a Holiday (no matter how minor): Luckily, my mom had lots of patience and loved to cook. We often had Valentine's parties (my sisters, and my friends and me) Super Bowl parties (for my brother and his friends) or Halloween parties (co-ed), where she would come up with games and serve us lots of food. It definitely kept us away from the "parents-are-away-for-the-weekend" parties that were going on.

6. Game Room: We had a friend whose parents had tons of board games, a ping pong table, an air hockey table, pinball machine, and a foosball table. This was awesome. It was great when it was just girls, or just boys, but also a great way to spend time with the opposite sex when they came over. You might think about getting one of these or some videogame systems, like a Wii with lots of controllers. My brother and his friends all had their own "laser-guns" and would wear vests and little blinking things and run around the neighborhood or back yards in their own version of outdoor laser tag.

7. Plan a Tournament: For boys, host a video game tournament at your house or, if you have the space or live near a park, have a sports day. For girls, I would also put spa party/sleepover, chocolate making party, and craft or jewelry-making party under this category.

8. Attend an event: Go to free outdoor concerts, big music festivals, or sports games.

9. House Hop: This one takes lots of coordination, but works really well if you do end up organizing a parent-event-planning-committee (above). Since teens get bored really easily, have four different families get together and host a different part of the night (preferably if they are in walking or short driving distance). One house does snacks and outdoor activities, then someone else has a BBQ dinner, someone else does game night, and then end with dessert.

10. Drop Off: There are lots of game centers, go-cart tracks, water parks, and theme parks where you can drop off a bunch of teens and maybe hang out in the area, have a date night while they play.

Note 1: Make sure your kids and their friends know that there is no drinking, sneaking away, or drugs at these events. My parents used to collect everyone's keys at the beginning of the night and make everyone say hello and goodbye to make sure they were in an okay state before they left.

*Note 2: I know this seems rough, but the whole point is to let teens feel like they are having fun and still having their independence so they do not need to get [attention] by rebelling. My parents were always home, but would go upstairs or stay in another room, only coming down if [our music] got too loud. They would not repeatedly check on us, because they trusted us. This, in turn, made us feels more responsible so we made sure we did not, nor did any of our friends, break the rules.

☼ **BE THE DIFFERENCE** ☼

Helping Others
by Eryn Gorang - age 18

I am drug free and don't intend to drink until I'm twenty-one, and then it will only be an occasional drink.

My family has always been involved with service, and I started very young, doing service projects through my church. The focus of my Community of Grace Presbyterian Church is to put your religion into action. I've been on a mission trip to Colorado, where we served the community working with a program for low-income families through the Salvation Army and the refugee center. One summer, I went with a youth group to Mexico and built a house for a low-income family in Tijuana, which is the center of poverty. The most life-changing experience was a mission trip to San Francisco. We went into the Tenderloin district, which is particularly known for poverty. We slept on the floor of the church, and every day we would go do a different service activity. One day our challenge was to see how we could use $20 to help people. We were told to go into People's Park and talk to the homeless. We talked to tons of people and gave out gift cards to Subway, Burger King, or McDonald's (still to this day, I always carry gift cards with me when I go downtown).

Kiwanis Key Club

I entered high school and knew I wanted to be part of a group which involved community service. That's when I joined Key Club. Some kids begin working with Kiwanis in junior high, through the Builders Club, but at that time there wasn't a junior high-level club available in my area.

- **What kind of activities have you been involved with in Kiwanis?**

When I entered the club my sophomore year, I wasn't very happy with the way it was set up because I like doing constant service. Because the Key Club wasn't as organized as I'd hoped, I ran for president in my junior year. We made scarves and hats for the battered women's shelter, and went to an elderly home and planned games and projects for them. We planned an entire homecoming dance and earned over $3000 that we could use for different relief projects, and we tutored local kids.

My favorite project was a Cystic Fibrosis Run Walk. We did everything from figuring out the running path, to getting sponsors to having raffles, having entertainment, and even making sure the janitors were there.

Through our hard work and persistence, we raised over $3000 for the Cystic Fibrosis Foundation. Two of my good friends from the volleyball team have cystic fibrosis, so this project had special meaning to me.

My senior year, I ran for Key Club Lieutenant Governor of the Utah Idaho District at their district convention. I won the election and that's what I've been doing all this year. Some of the highlights of my year include:

- Putting Key Clubs into East and Jordan High Schools.
- Creating Builders Clubs for junior high schools so the kids can get started much younger than I did.
- Planning District Convention, which is in March this year. They have lots of contests and awards.
- Last summer I went to the International Convention, which involved kids from Germany and Jamaica and all over the world who are a part of Key Club.

I try to fall asleep, but I keep thinking of all the things on my list I need to cross off. It has helped me organize my time.

• **How can others join Key Club?**

If there is a Key Club at your school, you just have to pay a small fee to enter, like $10, because it goes to the international group to help them do really big projects. If you don't have the money, they can waive the fee. Once you join, you come to all the meetings and do all the service projects.

If you don't have a Key Club, you can just find out who your local Kiwanian is and you can get a sponsor and start your own group, at your school. You can go to Key Club.org to find out all about that.

• **Why do you think kids should be involved with service clubs?**

Service makes you aware of other people outside of yourself. In our society, it's so easy to get carried away with me, me, me. But when you are in service, you open up to other people and you see the benefits of that work. It not only gives you this warm, fuzzy feeling but it's also making a small difference. As one person, I can't fix everything, but everyone should do what they can.

• **Will your service lead to scholarships?**

Key Club International has scholarships available. They give out five full-ride scholarships each year to Arizona State University. But that's not all—almost every Kiwanis club gives out a $1000 scholarship to the Key Club for the schools they sponsor, and they have all kinds of scholarships Key Club members can apply for on the district level and international level.

• **What are your plans for the future?**

I have always been in accelerated classes. In high school I became an International Bachelorette student, having my classes graded against students all over the world.

I've applied to nine colleges in Massachusetts, North Carolina, Ohio, California, and Utah. It will depend on which college I receive money to attend. I really want to go into business, communications, and public relations, and hopefully start my own non-profit organization or be really involved with one. I know that service is something I want to do and I want to do it in the most powerful way I can.

☼ **KNOW YOURSELF** ☼

MUSIC KEEPS ME FOCUSED
by Laura Damewood - age 17

• **Has anyone ever asked you to smoke, drink, or do drugs?**

I try to be a good example and sometimes I hang out with kids that I know do drugs. If drug use occurs, I leave immediately.

• **What are the main factors in your life that help you stay away from drugs?**

I never want to do drugs. I've seen what people do when they are high, and it's embarrassing. It helps that I'm involved with numerous activities. That way, I don't have the time to do drugs, and the people I'm around most of the time don't do drugs.

• **I know that you are a busy girl, with many interests. Can you name some of those interests?**

I'm involved in dancing, singing, 2 bands at school, theatre, running, piano, and the French horn.

• **How long have you been playing the piano?**

I've been playing the piano since I was five.

• **In what way do you think the piano has helped you with discipline for your other interests and activities?**

It takes a lot of concentration to make sure the notes come out right. It also takes a lot of concentration to play the piano for a whole hour each day. Playing the piano has required so much discipline that has carried over into every part of my life.

- **How much importance would you give music in your life and the life of your family?**

My family has classical music playing in the house most of the time. Music helps with brain function. If I'm doing homework, the music helps me study and remember for tests. I think the music needs to be classical, not rock music.

- **Can you tell me about the school band trip you have planned?**

I am going to New York in April to perform on Broadway with the cast of "Ragtime." We will be practicing for at least an hour a day with the cast to prepare for the show. Our band will be in costume with stage makeup. We perform for one night, and then we will appear on the CBS Morning Show, we will have a ticket for another Broadway play, and tour New York. I am so excited.

- **How much importance would you give religion in your life and the life of your family?**

Religion has helped a lot in my life. I have seen how some of my regular friends are tempted to do things that I would never do. With Christ in my life, I can keep myself morally clean and make better choices.

- **You are the youngest in your family. How important has the example of your older brother and sisters been to your choices?**

All my siblings have been involved in activities such as music. We all play the piano. Because of them, I have tried harder. I even chose running because no one else has been a runner and I don't have to outdo them in that area. I really think the examples of my older brother and two sisters have made me push harder.

- **Laura, you have been home schooled for much of your life. Did that put you ahead in school, or behind? Please explain.**

I was home schooled until I was in the seventh grade. When I went to public school, I was ahead in math. I started Pre-Algebra and went onto geometry. I then started Algebra 2 in high school.

- **What helped you adjust to public school?**

In the sixth grade I attended the Kennedy Junior High concert band to learn the French horn. Being at the junior high one hour a day helped me transition into public school, learn my way around, and meet some kids.

- **Do you think it was easier to stay away from bad influences because of you were not in public school?**

I grew up without having to deal with the social issues of public school. I had neighborhood friends, but only had to deal with the people I liked. My older brother and sisters helped prepare me for school by telling me stories. When I got to public school, I hung out with good kids but couldn't avoid the bad kids. Sometimes I had to change classes or move to a different seat.

- **I have noticed your work as a lifeguard at the West Valley Pool. Did you need special training to be a lifeguard?**

I took swimming lessons when I was younger. In order to be a lifeguard, I took one week of training and practiced saving people. Then we were required to train once a month to review and practice saving people. We had to practice until we got it right.

- **Your mom said that you work hard all summer so you can afford to do your extra activities. What are those activities?**

Working as a lifeguard, I earned enough money to pay for the band tour, my socks and shoes for running, and everything else I needed for my extra activities, including my dress for Madrigals—

my singing group at school. My dress cost $150 and I paid for it myself.

- **Laura, you are a junior this year. What are your plans for the future?**

I plan to take biology and anatomy, and then go into physical therapy. I want to be a physical therapist, because I saw how much it helped my mom after a car accident. I really want to help people.

☼ BE TRUE ☼

My Path to Success
by Devon Green - age 18

When I was 5 years old, I started my own business called "Devon's Heal the World." I recycled for over 100 local businesses in my home town of Stuart, Florida. By the age of 15, I had raised over ¼ million dollars for various national and international charities.

These past thirteen years, my efforts not only assisted those less fortunate than myself, but it afforded me the opportunity to progress in my own life skills and career. By becoming involved with community service at such a young age, I developed a level of responsibility that is not seen in most teenagers. Charitable giving is self-motivated; no one forced me to do it. This turned me into a better student, as my teachers and parents did not have to stand over me in order for me to do my work. I just did what had to be done, as with charity work. Due to my successful work ethic, I was able to immediately enroll in classes at my local community college when I graduated from middle school. Now, at the age of 18, I have earned my Bachelor's Degree in Business Administration & Law and am currently looking into Master's Degree programs.

While I have accomplished a great deal at an early age, all that I have achieved would not have been possible had I become involved with drugs or alcohol. When I graduated from eighth grade, I left the private Christian school that I had attended since the age of two and stepped into the state college system by registering as a home schooled high school student and taking dual enrollment classes at Indian River State College in Florida.

Though I did not attend a typical high school, I did keep in touch with a number of my friends from middle school, and I met other high school students through them and in turn met more high school students as well. This continuous pattern led me to become acquainted with a number of high school students with whom I became very social.

Initially, I did not encounter any issues. If anything, the most difficult hurdle for me to overcome was my shy nature. I had attended a school where I progressed all the way from kindergarten to eighth grade with practically the same twenty students in my class. Once I began meeting new people, I discovered the thrill of socializing with a wide variety of different peers, and I was hooked! I began going to movies, parties, and other social events with a number of different individuals and groups of kids. I was so attached to my new-found fun that I was willing to do almost anything to ensure its survival. I conformed to practically every group of people that I met. I made the choice to become involved in a number of different things that didn't really interest me, such as video games, anime, etc. I liked to watch crime shows that solved cold cases and I read mystery novels, but I began to watch and to read things that my new acquaintances liked just to ensure that I would have things to talk about with them. While my classmates and I were all basically stuck with each other throughout elementary and middle school, my new friends were not stuck with me because there were plenty of other high school students who could be their friends if they decided that they did not like me. For the first time, I understood what it was like to feel the need to conform in order to fit in. I felt peer pressure, and, in my opinion, that is one of the main reasons that kids become involved with drugs and alcohol. It's the reason that I almost did.

I attended parties and social events with my friends for nearly a year without any damaging peer pressure. I watched a few movies that I didn't like, read a few books that didn't interest me, and picked out a few shirts that didn't flatter me, but I was not pressured to do anything destructive.

However, one evening I was staying over at a friend's house in the same neighborhood where a mutual friend of ours was having a party. When the time came for the party to start, my friend Naomi and I walked to our friend's house. When we first arrived, I was unaware that anything was not as I expected. A few other friends had arrived and were watching a couple of people play a game of pool out on the back porch. Naomi and I found chairs on the porch, ate pretzels, and laughed it up with the other party attendees. About fifteen minutes later, one of the kids brought a pack of beer out of the fridge and started passing them around. It was then that it became obvious to Naomi and me that there were no parents in the house and that the party was about to turn into a drinking event. At that point, we had a couple of different options: we could drink with the rest of our friends and fit in, or leave the party and be the only two people who didn't fit in. After a moment of whispered discussion, we told everyone else at the party that Naomi's mom had given us a curfew, and then we left. We didn't drink and I never went back.

Naomi was by my side, and that's what made me feel confident in walking out of the party that night. If Naomi had decided to stay and to drink, I know that I would have ended up staying in an uncomfortable situation. Kids would have been offering me drinks all night and making fun of me if I didn't take them. Whether I would have ended up drinking that night, I cannot say. I hope I would have made the right choice, but without anyone on my side, I'm not sure if I would have buckled under the pressure.

If I had started drinking that night, the path that followed would likely have been a downward spiral. I would have begun to travel further and further away from the path and the people who led me to the success, the education, and the life that I have today. Looking back with the knowledge of who I am and where I am right now, I am proud of myself for deciding not to become involved with drugs or alcohol when I was tempted. I like who I have become, and I am truly thankful to my family, to my true friends like Naomi, and to God for giving me the strength to be an individual instead of just another one of the crowd.

☼ You Can ☼

Be a Leader
by Dallan Carter - age 18

Choosing Friends with Good Values

As a new sophomore at Hillcrest High School in Salt Lake City, Utah, I decided that I would have no regrets in high school. I wanted to be able to walk across the stage at graduation, think about my time at Hillcrest, and say to myself, "I did it all. I took every opportunity to succeed in a worthwhile cause, and I ran with it.

I have no regrets." I knew it wouldn't be easy, but I set about it by taking small steps.

The first and most important factor to my well-being in high school was my choice of friends. While everyone has the choice to act according to their own standards, we tend to give in to what our closest buddies are doing, whether it is good or bad. These are the steps I took to ensure that drugs wouldn't enter into my daily life:

1. The people I spent every waking hour with were the type of people who would never allow that into their own lives, let alone offer it to someone else.

2. I lived my life in such a way that the kids who were involved with drugs and alcohol knew what my answer would be long before asking. I never shunned those kids—in fact, I feel like I was equally warm and caring to everyone around me regardless of their decisions. I just know that they would never bother to ask me because of my evident character traits.

By the end of the year, I noticed I had never been offered drugs or alcohol. To this day, I give all the credit to my friends for working with me to entirely shut out such negative behaviors.

Peer Leadership Team

At the end of my sophomore year, I tried out for the prestigious Peer Leadership Team. I made the team! I was one of thirty members of the new Hillcrest Peer Leadership Team. An excited but nervous junior, I soon learned why being a part of this team is so important. It's all about service, and preventing drug and alcohol abuse and violence in young children who will soon be responsible for the world around us.

We spent the first quarter of my junior year visiting elementary schools to teach sixth graders how to effectively say no to bad activities. The second and third quarter, each team member was paired up with a student (grades 4-6) from Oakdale Elementary to teach him or her better reading habits and strategies. After we said our goodbyes to our tutees from Oakdale, we spent the fourth quarter re-visiting the sixth grade students from numerous elementary schools to refresh old information as well as presenting them with suggestions about how to deal with and prevent bullying.

Teaching Refusal Skills

Before the time came for PLT to visit schools in the fall and spring, we separated into our pre-determined teams and we practiced the entire presentation from beginning to end, using the other two teams as imaginary sixth graders. We had to make sure we knew exactly what we were doing and how to respond to a real audience.

Once we were in the classroom, we did an intro, explanation of why we were there, presentation of the rules, and then we would tell them about the five Peer Refusal Skills. Each student was given a card with the list of skills so they could follow along and keep it for future reference. Once we read and explained each skill, the selected team members would act out a role play to demonstrate that skill. Five Peer Leadership members stood in order, each with an overturned poster with one skill written on it.

The Five Peer Refusal Skills (and their key phrases in parentheses) are:

1) **Ask questions** (Who will be there? What are we going to do? Why would I do that?)

2) **Name the trouble** (That's... (illegal, bad, cheating, etc.))

3) **State the consequence** (If I do that, then... (I could get grounded; I could go to detention etc.))

4) **Suggest an alternative** (Instead, why don't we get together at my house and watch a movie, go bowling etc.?)

5) **Move it, sell it, and leave the door open** (I'm going to go _____, if you change your mind, you can come too! [then physically walk away from them])

When visiting a classroom, one member plays a bad guy and asks if we want to cheat, steal, or smoke pot. The first skill is demonstrated with the question, "Why would I want to do that?" Each member of the team has a part in acting out a scene and demonstrating each of the five refusal skills. The students identify which skill has been demonstrated by holding up a finger. After we act out the skills, team members divide the class into small groups and help them act out their own role play of refusal skills in front of the class, which they love. The PLT team leads the group in a cool-down activity (making rain with our hands and feet). We then invite the members to come up to the front so the students can ask us questions about middle school, high school, sports, hobbies, etc.

The kids love having us come. They look up to us a lot, because we are older, tall, and smart, but not adults. So they will listen to us and learn what we are teaching them.

Other Accomplishments in High School

Although PLT may seem very time consuming, it all took place during our 8th period, which comes only every other day. This left me with plenty of time to do what I pleased.

- I tried out for and acquired a sub-lead role in the fall musical, which requires a lot of commitment and time.
- I was enrolled in two rigorous AP classes and several other intense Honors courses.
- I often attended after-school rehearsals for concert choir in preparation for the state competition or an upcoming concert.
- I decided to apply and campaign for student body president. With lots of work and campaigning, I was able to earn this valued office

for my senior year of high school.

• I valued spending time with my close friends or attending well-planned parties.

• Virtually any free time I had was spent asleep. If I was awake, I was doing something productive.

I can't believe how quickly my senior year flew by—I surrounded myself with friends just like me; they were all just as involved, just as driven to succeed, and just as wise with their time and decisions. Thankfully, I still have not been offered drugs or alcohol, nor have I participated by my own accord in such an activity.

Recently, I was able to walk across the stage at graduation, dressed in a green cap and gown. I had a big smile on my face. Guess what my thoughts were?

"I did it all. I took every opportunity to succeed in a worthwhile cause, and I ran with it. *I have no regrets.*"

My Plans for the Future

I plan to serve a two-year LDS mission after completing the fall semester at BYU in Provo, Utah. After my mission, I will pursue a degree in whatever field is best—I haven't decided between Civil Engineering and Optometry. Because of my ACT test scores, along with a high GPA, I qualified for the Heritage Scholarship, which provides me with four years of full tuition, paid by BYU.

A World of Opportunities

☼ Find Your Path ☼

See the World
by Lina Gassner - age 19
from Hamburg, Germany
Exchange Student to Perrsburg, Ohio in 2007-2008

When I was sixteen, I became an exchange student to the U.S. It wasn't necessary to have the best grades; however it was helpful for me to know English. I had studied English in school ever since the fifth grade. The cost to be an exchange student was $7000, but I got a $5000 scholarship. The host parents are volunteers. Kids from Germany have gone to several different countries, such as Italy, Canada, Korea, and down to South America.

My host family in Ohio included my host parents, an older brother and sister, a brother my age, plus a younger brother. I was a teenager so I didn't always get along with the host mother but I really like the family.

When I went to my new school, I was like a celebrity. I was even friends with the most popular kids. My passion is soccer, and in the spring I started to play soccer for a fun team, where the girls were all my age. We had soccer games each weekend. Because I hadn't used English as my first language, there were many words I didn't understand. For instance: The couch said, "When you hear the whistle blow, run, run, run." I understood, run, run, run, but "What's a whistle?" My team began the word of the day. Every day they taught me a new word. I can learn languages very well, especially because I took four years of Latin, in Germany. Before I left the U.S., no one could tell I was from Germany. They could only hear a slight accent, but they weren't sure where the accent was from.

I was different when I returned to Germany. I was more mature. When I looked around at the other students in my class, I could tell somehow which kids had been exchange students and which had not, because those who didn't leave the country were still the same.

Becoming an Exchange Student:

The application process begins 4-10 months before you begin the program. Host families volunteer to take students and pay for food and transportation. Students usually provide health insurance, and clothing. Some programs require a student to have some use of the language before being accepted.

Who do I contact?
• Rotary Youth Exchange offers summer exchange or academic exchange. Rotary International provides scholarships. www.rotaryyouthexchange.net
• Youth for Understanding: YFU is a non-profit educational organization which offers opportunities for young people around the world to spend a summer, semester or year with a host family in another culture. www.yfu.org
• AFS--offers school exchanges in more than 50 countries across the globe, or you can choose a summer exchange. www.afs.org

☼ BUILD ON YOUR STRENGTHS ☼

THE CAPTAIN OF MY LIFE
by Debora Hollomon - age 22

I am doing what I like. I have worked on the whale watch boat, the Scotch Mist II, for one year. Prior to living and working on Maui, Hawaii, I was a flight attendant. Then I went to work for an inter-island airline in Hawaii. When I went sailing for the first time, I knew I had found the life I loved. I quit my job working for the airline and got hired on with the Scotch Mist II as an assistant to the captain. Now I wasn't only working at what I loved—I was living my dream. Since I have worked on the sailing boat for one year now, after only two more years, I will have my captain's license and be able to sail anywhere I want.

Gene, the captain of the Scotch Mist II, is training Debbie. "She works hard with the sails. I'm getting older, and I really depend on her," he said of the small framed girl, about 5'5" and under 115 lbs. "She's capable of doing the work of turning the sails and steering the boat."

Debbie, after you become a captain, will you have your own boat?

I may own a boat someday, but it costs so much, and it requires a lot of work. For now, I want to be a captain of other people's boats.

It is also very expensive to live in Hawaii, but I think it's worth it to sacrifice for what is really important to you. I work two jobs. Besides working on the boat, I work for an organic/vegan food store in town. I only have one day off per week.

Will you settle down and get married someday?

I'm not sure, but for now, my motto is: No pets, no kids, and no boyfriends. I don't want anything to get in the way of my goal to be a captain.

My mother is hoping for grandchildren, and my grandparents, who live in Virginia, ask what's next for me when I tire of "this little adventure." But sailing is all I want to do.

Although the passengers of a boat may drink, captains of seafaring vessels have to be drug and alcohol free.

I am very goal oriented, but I have lost a lot of friends because of alcohol. I feel that alcohol and drugs will get in the way of your life and living your dreams.

☼ **BUILD YOUR DREAMS** ☼

SEEING THE WORLD THROUGH A CAMERA
by Georgina - age 23

I am a photographer on the Princess Cruises, Golden Princess cruise ship. I'm under an eight-month contract and this is my second contract. My home is in Wales, where I earned a degree in Photography. I have wanted to be a photographer since I was fifteen. To achieve my goal, I worked hard in school and took photography classes in high school. Next, I got a job in a photo shop. I knew that wasn't enough for me, so I went on to take three years of photography in college. Now I'm living my dream, taking photos on the ship. I make as much money as I would be making at a regular eight-hour-a-day, forty-hour-a-week job at home—but I get to travel. I have room and board paid on the ship, so all the money I make is profit. I also met my partner on the ship.

Before this job, I worked for a cruise ship between New Zealand and Australia and stopped at the small islands in between. Now, I get to visit the islands of Hawaii on my days off. This ship will go to Hawaii for several months, and then switch to Alaska during the summer.

Working for a cruise ship, you get to travel, and see the world—you get to meet people from all over.

What would you like to tell kids about your job and following your dream?

I want to tell kids what a great life they can have, traveling around the world. On a cruise ship, you can find a job you like—taking pictures, doing hair, massage, or even working in a daycare center. You can train for some of these jobs in high school. Then you can start traveling and doing what you love.

I am drug free. I have never taken drugs and I don't smoke. I would never do that. Living my life, doing what I want, and traveling are much better. With drugs, none of this would be possible for me.

QUESTIONS FOR TEENS

Do you have a plan in case you are approached with drugs?
Has anyone approached you with drugs, alcohol, or tobacco?
What did/will you do?
Why?
Can you avoid drug use, or have you tried drugs/alcohol or tobacco?
What would you tell others who are in the same situation?
Do the kids you hang out with smoke?
Do they drink on weekends?
Do you ever feel uncomfortable around kids you grew up with who are making different choices?
Can you tell them no?
Can you avoid them?
Will they tease you, confuse you, or pressure you to try something you really don't want to try?
Is there someone you can talk to about this?
Please find someone to talk to if you are having a hard time saying no.

Conclusion: Drugs Make You Un-Smarter
by Savanna Peterson - age 15

When I found out about weed, I was eight. My mom used to smoke it, and when I would smell it coming out of the bathroom, I would just go into my room and cry. The first time I saw weed with my own eyes was when I was ten. My brother and his girlfriend Trisha were in the garage smoking weed from a pop can made into a pipe. I have been around drugs and alcohol my whole life, and I choose not to follow. I choose to be a leader. Being a leader feels much better.

Most people who do drugs now saw someone taking it and thought that person was cool. They were offered a drug and probably rejected it the first time. They didn't feel cool, so they eventually tried it, got screwed up, and became addicted. But the lucky ones tried it and thought it was horrible and never did it again.

Doing drugs at a young age will lead to bad grades, loss of trust, and loss of money. I hope my words will teach others and help people with their future so they don't end up flipping hamburgers at McDonald's. This may be a good job for a teenager, but isn't what you should be doing when you're an adult.

Doing drugs may be fun for awhile, but in time you will see what it can do to your body. You may breakout in zits or have bad teeth, lose a lot of weight, and be 'un-smarter,' meaning to become dumber—especially from missing school and hanging around jerks who do drugs. You won't have a good life.

People who do Ecstasy are called "E-tards" because they've lost their mind from taking too many pills. Smoking weed can increase your hunger and make you useless, if used 24/7. Alcohol addiction can make you change into an angry person. It makes you forget, blame others, and lose control. It can also cause accidents in the home and in the car.

When you meet a guy/girl at a party, at first you may think he or she is really cool. But once you realize you have fallen in love with a person who drinks or does drugs, you may realize their life is going nowhere.

Why should you have to waste your life doing drugs and going to parties when you can have a better future? Maybe the person you fell in love with doesn't have a future, but you do! Stop while you can. Graduate from high school, go to college or vocational training, and get a good job. Parties are always there. But at some point, you're going to get older and the people you party with will be homeless because their parents were sick of their laziness and not being able to trust them.

I am telling you this because I care. I really do. And I want to help. Trust me; you do not want to share your life with the broke, drugged-out forty-year-old guy who still thinks he's seventeen. He's always going to be like that. Going with a guy who does drugs or doing drugs yourself will not lead you anywhere. Yeah, maybe it will give you friends, but later on you will find them on the street looking for change to buy whatever put them there in the first place. Help your friends quit! Look at what's in your hands—something called disappointment. Don't choose drugs or drinking over family, because in the end, they're all you've got. Losing friends is nothing. Losing family or trust is everything.

CONTRIBUTORS TO
DRUGS MAKE YOU UN SMARTER

Erica Catton has dedicated the last 9 years to helping those struggling with drugs and alcohol. She is currently working for Narconon Arrowhead as an Executive over the promotion, marketing, and public relations areas. She continues to live her life every day to help others who are struggling through the ravages of drug and alcohol addiction.

Tray Chaney has been on stage as a dancer since age four. He stepped into acting with the role of "Poot" on the Peabody-winning HBO drama series, "The Wire." Tray continued with "The Wire" for five consecutive seasons.

As well as acting, Tray has performed on music videos and recently began taping his debut album.

Tray Chaney is the author of his autobiography "The Truth You Can't BeTray", Tray has long been an advocate for reading and literacy. He has joined with a group of celebrities in the Write Stuff Literacy Campaign to promote reading to school-age children.

Sherry Gaba, LCSW, is a licensed psychotherapist and life coach. Sherry appears monthly as a guest expert on the radio show, Dr. Drew Live, and she was seen in action on VH1's Celebrity Rehab 2 and 3. As a life coach, Sherry helped cast members make a transition on the spin-off Sober House. Sherry is currently involved with the 2111 production, Celebrity Rehab 4.

Sherry Gaba's latest book, "The Law of Sobriety, Attracting Positive Energy for a Powerful Recovery" about recovery from addictions and alcoholism, is now available through HCI publishing, http://sherrygaba.hcibooks.com.

Brooks Gibbs, Youth Motivational Speaker, grew up in a dysfunctional family shattered by divorce and addiction. He turned his story into a tale of life transformation.

Brooks Gibbs has earned a reputation as a leading authority on the youth issues of bullying and life choices. Featured in,Teen People Magazine, Washington Post and interviewed on CBS, his inspiring personal stories and helpful strategies have reached more than a million teens and counting.

For more information or to book Brooks Gibbs for your next function, visit: www.brooksgibbs.com

Devon Green is the founder of Devon's Heal the World Recycling, which she started when she was five years old. Her younger sister, Jessica Green, is the Vice President of Recycling. The business includes giving of her time and raising funds to help others, as well as helping the planet.

Eighteen-year-old Devon has completed her Bachelor's Degree in Business at Western Carolina University and plans to attend graduate school.

The story of Devon's Heal the World Recycling has been featured in newspapers and magazines around the world and in textbooks read by children in the Netherlands.

Kevin Hauschulz, has been in recovery for 3 years. As the lead Telephone Recovery Support Coordinator for the Connecticut Community for Addiction Recovery, Kevin attempts to reach out to people in recovery and provide them with recovery support services, as well as putting on trainings in many different subject areas.

Kevin has a degree in Psychology and an Associate's Degree in Drug and Alcohol Recovery Counseling. Kevin currently is enrolled at Springfield College in their School of Social Work. Kevin hopes to attain his Licensed Alcohol and Drug Counseling Certification (LADC) in the near future.

Punyamurtula Kishore M.D., M.P.H., is the medical director of Preventive Medicine Associates in Brookline, MA.

Dr. Kishore began his medical career as a primary care/family practice physician and then moved into a position as the Medical Director of the Washingtonian Center for Addiction, the first organization in the U.S. to recognize addiction as a disease. Dr. Kishore has been a member of the American Society of Addiction Medicine since 1986 and has helped treat more than 140,000 addicts.

In 1993, Dr. Kishore founded National Library of Addictions in Brookline, Massachusetts. The Library is designed to provide a non-profit structure for addiction professionals to exchange ideas and to further the development of treatment methodologies.

Kristen Moeller, MS, is an author, coach, speaker, and radio show host.

After suffering for years with an eating disorder and drug addiction, Kristen Moeller discovered that she was always waiting for something to change. She finally realized that the change needed to come from within herself. In 2008, Kristen wrote the bestseller, "Waiting for Jack," which was picked up by a major New York Agent and has a forward written by Jack Canfield. Kristen is the celebrity ambassador for the National Eating Disorder Association, and works for her own non-profit organization, The Chick-a-go Foundation, providing pay-it-forward scholarships to transformational educational events. www.waitingforjack.com

Mikey Rox is an award-winning journalist/writer and the principal of a media management and marketing company called Paper Rox Scissors. He is a 2003 graduate of Roanoke College, where he earned a

B.A. degree in English and a minor in Spanish. His professional work has appeared in more than 100 regional, national, and international print and online publications throughout North America and Europe. Rox currently resides in New York City with his fiancé and their dog, Jaxon.

Jennifer Storm has degrees in Rehabilitation Services and Organizational Management and a certificate of Human Resources Dispute Management and Resolution. Ms. Storm joined the Victims' Witness Assistance Program, VWAP, as the organization's second Executive Director. In 2002, Pennsylvania Governor Edward G. Rendell appointed Ms. Storm as a commissioner to the Pennsylvania Commission on Crime and Delinquency.

Ms. Storm is the author of two personal memoirs—"Blackout Girl: Growing Up and Drying Out in America" (Hazelden 2008) and "Leave the Light On: A Memoir of Recovery and Self-Discovery" (Central Recovery Press 2010), both which chronicle her own journey as a rape survivor and her 10-year battle with drug addiction and alcoholism.

Vanessa Van Petten, age 25, is the author of the parenting book "You're Grounded!" She founded RadicalParenting.com where she gives her expertise, along with 60 teen writers, ages 12-20, to help parents and adults get an honest and open view into the world and mind of youth.

Parents learn to better understand their teenager and kids grasp the importance of social literacy to prevent bullying, cliques, and miscommunication with their parents.

Radicalparenting.com is read by thousands of teens and parents daily, and Vanessa was chosen as one of the top 100 Bloggers to watch by Women Magazine.

Vanessa has been featured in teen magazines, newspapers and television shows giving a young perspective on awesome parenting. Van Petten is now on an international speaking tour.

Dr. Talia Witkowski is an addictions and eating disorder specialist. Dr. Talia learned about these afflictions through her own suffering. She has put her expertise to work in treatment centers and private practice with people with eating disorders and addictions. She received healing without the use of diets, exercise regimes, medication, or traditional psychotherapy (or having to enter into a residential treatment program). Help came to her from a custom-tailored lifestyle program called "Heal Your Hunger." She is now the Marketing and Outreach Coordinator of this incredible organization. If you have any questions, please reach out: Talia@HealYourHunger.com.

About the Authors

Savanna Peterson, nicknamed Bab Sav because she is less than five feet tall, is a tenth-grader from Utah. Her favorite thing to do is ghost hunting with friends. Her favorite band is Sleeping Giant. Her favorite movies are The Sandlot and Stand by Me. Savanna's favorite food is chicken taco salad.

Savanna says, "I try to have as much fun as I possibly can, and that doesn't include drugs or drinking. You have more fun when you can remember your memories. I like to remember what I did the night before.

"I spend all my time wisely. I want to be an archeologist when I am older. I'm very open-minded and kind. I have a heart and I show it most of the time, but I just can't tolerate seeing people mess up their lives with drugs."

The authors keep a blog at:
DrugsMakeYouUnSmarter.blogspot.com
and Savanna appears with her grandmother in a short book trailer: Through the Rug 2: Follow that Dog on YouTube.

Jill Vanderwood is Savanna's grandmother and the author of four children's books. She is the winner of the 2008 Writer of the Year Award from the League of Utah Writers.

Jill has witnessed firsthand how drugs affect a family through marriage to an alcoholic and the drug addiction of several family members.

Jill's book, *What's It Like, Living Green? Kids Teaching Kids by the Way They Live*, is the First Place Winner of three national book awards and won second place on a state level. Through her book sales, she has been an active fundraiser for the Literacy Action Center in Salt Lake City, Wheelchair Foundation, the Hibiscus Children's Center in Florida, and the Southwind Sustainable Park, in Springfield, IL.

Jill Vanderwood also appears in the documentary film, Achieve Your Ultimate Success, available at a bookstore near you. You can find more information about Drugs Make You Un-Smarter at: **www.jillvanderwood.com**

Other books by Jill Ammon Vanderwood

- Through the Rug
- Through the Rug 2: Follow That Dog
- Stowaway: The San Francisco Adventures of Sara the Pineapple Cat
- What's It Like, Living Green? Kids Teaching Kids By the Way They Live

www.ingramcontent.com/pod-product-compliance
Lightning Source LLC
LaVergne TN
LVHW051045080426
835508LV00019B/1712